# HOW TO KNOW AND CHOOSE YOUR MEN THROUGH PALMISTRY

**Mary Fasulis**

WARNER BOOKS

A Warner Communications Company

Warner Books Edition

Copyright © 1983, 1984 by Maria Loison Fasulis

This book was originally published under the title, *How to Choose Your Men Through Palmistry.* A special chapter about how to read your own hands has been added for this edition.

This Warner Books edition is published by arrangement with the author.

Warner Books, Inc., 666 Fifth Avenue, New York, NY 10103

W A Warner Communications Company

Printed in the United States of America
First Warner printing: October 1984
10 9 8 7 6 5 4 3 2 1

Cover design by Barbara Buck    Cover photos by Daniel Wagner

*Disclaimer:* Actions taken based upon the ideas and suggestions and statements contained in this book are done at the sole risk of the reader.

**Library of Congress Cataloging in Publication Data**

Fasulis, Mary.
  How to know and choose your men through palmistry.
  Originally published: How to choose your men through palmistry. 1st ed. Sacramento, CA: M. Fasulis, c1983. With a new chapter.
  1. Mate selection. 2. Men—Psychology. 3. Palmistry. I. Title.
BF935.M35F37  1984        133.6            84-7258
ISBN 0-446-38113-6 (pbk.) (USA)
     0-446-38114-4 (pbk.) (Canada)

MARY FASULIS is a hand analyst who has been studying hand reading extensively since 1965 and possesses a wide range of knowledge on this subject. She has read for and advised hundreds of people from all walks of life in the United States and Europe. She writes articles for magazines and has spoken on several radio programs in the United States and Canada.

To my friends who encouraged me to write this book and to the hundreds of men and women who came to me for readings.

**THANK YOU**

---

**To**

**JOHN and LOUIS**

**YOU ARE STILL REMEMBERED AND LOVED**

---

**This book is written for men and women who want to know.....**

**SUCCESS**

**MONEY**

**LOVE**

**and**

**SEX.**

# CONTENTS

# FOREWORD

My purpose in writing this book is to share with you the knowledge that I have acquired on the ancient science of hand analysis.

Reading this book will give you new insights into evaluating and understanding the important men in your life — your father, your son, your husband and/or your lover.

The book offers just what the title says — a better way to choose your men using a scientific method that is as old as man.

MARY FASULIS

# I. INTRODUCTION

In the beginning God created man, God created woman, and the mating game began. Eve accepted the game centuries ago before she placed Adam under her spell with the trickery we women use so well.

Eve, of course, didn't have the choices we women have today, but then neither did Adam.

At least there was a balance in the early stages of our seductive and reproductive development. Today we women, unfortunately, have the numerical edge. This means the competition for even the most mediocre specimens could get pretty fierce.

That's partially why I've written this book — to give you an added advantage when you begin searching for big game.

The first thing you have to do before setting your sights on any one man is to determine if he is really what he appears to be. Of course, if you're really desperate, that really won't matter. That's where this book will come in handy.

If you read the book carefully and learn your lessons well, you'll be able to know him better than he knows himself. Then and only then are you ready for serious games.

Each chapter will tell you more about unraveling the true him by using your eyes and the simple subterfuge of caressing his hand. You gain advantage after advantage and he remains in blissful ignorance while you compile a mental dossier of his pluses and minuses. It might be a bit underhanded, but remember you're playing for high stakes.

It won't take you more than a few pages to realize that every part and every position of every part of the hand can tell you something important about your man's character.

Palmistry, after all, is a science — an exact science. It has been around long before recorded history, though its acceptance has been cyclical.

Each line, each mount, each finger is symptomatic of his nature. The symptoms are as recognizable to the knowledgeable as disease symptoms are recognizable to your family doctor.

I want to turn you into a capable diagnostician by initiating you into a new, rather strange, and fantastic world. It's a world where you can determine a man's past, present and future with a few touches of the hand.

As impossible as it might seem, you can determine a man's longevity by his life line, his sexual capacity by the size of his Mount of Venus, his career potential by his Mount of Jupiter and the sizes of the phalanges on his fingers.

See, I told you it was a new world — even the words are new. It will be easy to learn what mounts and phalanges mean in the terms of a flesh and blood man in the chapters to come.

The fingers, the thumb, the mounts, and each individual line will take on a new meaning and offer you new perspectives into human nature as you absorb what I have learned during hundreds of private readings and hours of study.

Don't panic if you find a bad sign on his hand. It can

easily be offset by a counterbalancing sign. Remember you have to look at the hand in its entirety, not just the separate parts.

I want you to use the knowledge packed into this book to carefully choose the men who will share your life, even if it's only for a few stolen hours. Who wants a guy who kisses and tells? I want to tell you who to play fun and games with and who to avoid.

Love and sex — how do you determine which it is or even which it should be, if you don't really know the man? I guarantee you palmistry will let you know the man. If you're really brave, it can even let you know yourself.

Maybe that's the primary reason for my book — the fact that I've comforted too many women who are physically and mentally broken because they chose the wrong man.

This book won't keep you from making mistakes — that, ultimately, is up to you and possibly your destiny line. It will give you fair warning if danger lurks in a man's hand — the rest is up to you. So, read, learn and enjoy — the book and MEN.

# II. YOU

are about to begin a marvelous adventure, as you dig into the psyches of the men in your life by discovering the secrets that lie in the palms of their hands.

Before you begin looking at others, you will be better prepared if you search out the secrets in your own hands.

How can you possibly decide which man you want, if you know too little about yourself? Too often we begin our search at the wrong place, looking for answers in others, rather than in ourselves.

Don't be afraid of what you might find. Remember this is an adventure. Take each of your hands and examine it carefully. You may be surprised at the number of lines that crisscross each hand like a roadmap (Fig. A, page 8).

Actually that's what your palm is — a roadmap to your life. Like a roadmap, there are no secrets in your hands if you know how to read the straight and twisting lines and the pads of flesh (called mounts) that gently swell below your fingers.

In all honesty, you've probably never looked at your hands this closely before. They've been something to wash, cream, or dry rather than a guide to your past, present, and future. You've probably paid more attention to manicuring and polishing your nails than to the trails meandering across the hills and valleys of your palms.

It's time to change all that! Today you enter a new world — a world called palmistry. As you unlock the secrets that you hold in your own two hands, you'll better be able to understand events that have happened in your dealings with people — especially men.

Your hands, your thumbs, your fingers — each hold delicious secrets about you. Long before you hit a normal milestone in a relationship, discovering these secrets is a must if you are to understand why the relationship is doomed to be a failure or a rocket burst of success.

For example, if you have a strong head line, indicating high intelligence, and you expect that same degree of intelligence in a mate, you can check out a prospect's head line before chemistry takes over and destroys reason.

The length of your fingers will tell you if you're meticulous or a spur-of-the-moment person. The length will tell you the same thing about HIM. Things like that are important. It isn't easy for a slow, methodical person to adjust to one with a more mercurial nature. The longer the relationship lasts, the more difficult it becomes.

Long fingers are also another connotation of intelligence. If you have both long fingers and a strong head line, it is a sure bet that an intellectually stimulating gentleman is a must for the long run.

The fingers hold many more character traits, and they are outlined in detail in Chapter 3. Simply change the HE's to YOU. The results are the same, whether looking at a man's hand or your own.

The thumb is another sure giveaway to character. The larger your thumb, the more likely you are to value reason over emotion. It means you're strong and forceful, no namby-pamby to be walked over by a macho character who always has to have the last word.

If your thumb has a degree of flexibility, it will soften the iron rod which runs the length of many a large thumb. The stiff-thumbed woman, like the stiff-thumbed man, is stable and predictable — so don't plan to be the life of the party! Read Chapter 4 on thumbs carefully, then remember what you find.

While you are learning the secrets in your palms and fingers, remember that one line or part of the hand can always offset another part. Don't be too quick to judge yourself on others. Look at the hand as a whole, rather than at the individual parts when you begin assembling the pieces of who you are.

Perhaps the strongest individual indicators of your vices and virtues are the seven fleshy pads of muscle located at the base of your fingers and the sides of your palm.

The best way to explore these miniature hills is through touch. The best hands are those where the mounts are of equal size, because they show a well-balanced person. Don't be surprised if your hand tells you that you've missed the boat on this one. Most people do.

Each mount represents a different character trait. A pronounced Mount of Jupiter (see figure A, page 8, and the diagram in Chapter 5) means you're on a power trip and have to be in control. The power plays may be at work, in politics, or in bed. Bed is very important to the sexy lady with the very pronounced Mount of Jupiter.

Being sexy doesn't mean you hop from bed to bed, especially if you find a man with a matching Mount of Jupiter and a large Mount of Venus. You are a loyal lover, albeit a sometimes overbearing one, and you expect the same degree of loyalty from your mate.

Do you possess a pronounced Mount of Saturn? Then you've added one more intellectual symbol to a strong head line and a large, inflexible thumb.

Located at the base of the middle finger, the Mount of

Saturn shows intellectual ability. If the mount is well developed, you are a deep thinker with a tendency to be cynical and distrustful of your friends and lovers.

Each mount is meaningful, based on the degree of development. Read Chapter 5 carefully, as you explore the seven mounts on your own hands. Understanding the relationship of these fleshy mounts is critical to understanding why you respond to people and situations in a specific way.

You will need to read the entire book to adequately understand yourself as a person. Until you understand yourself — the real self — locked in the boundaries established by the lines in your hands, the mounts on your palms, and the size and shape of your fingers — you cannot hope to understand the secrets locked in the hands of the men in your life.

You must first know yourself through palmistry, and accept that self, before you begin searching for the perfect mate with those deceptively simple strokes of the hand.

Once you know and accept who you are, then you can begin to sort out the characteristics that are important to you, as a woman who knows herself. Once you've defined the character traits that are important to you, then you can begin your tactile search for a man.

I cannot guarantee that chemistry will not take over and wipe out your carefully laid plans. It is up to you to make that final decision. I have given you the tools to understand yourself and your needs as a woman. It is up to you to decide if you are willing to use those tools wisely to sift the wheat from the chaff!

# THE ROADMAP OF YOUR LIFE

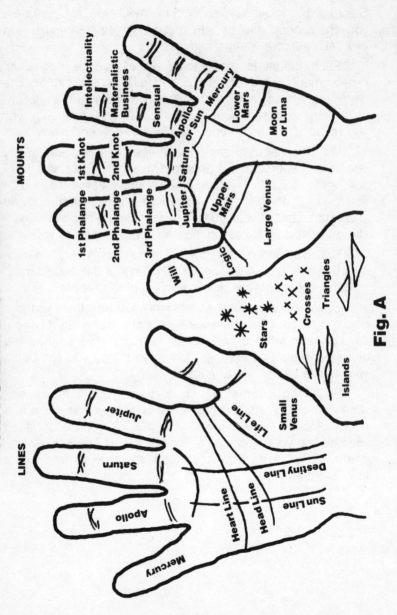

Fig. A

# THE RIGHT AND LEFT HANDS

It is very important to mention the difference between the right and left hand. The left hand shows all the traits of your personality and tendencies for disease which you inherited from your ancestors.

The right hand shows your successes, failures, achievements, events, or mistakes for which **you** are responsible. When you start your reading, place the two hands close together and examine all the lines and marks in both hands.

If a person is right handed, rely on the right hand, if left handed, rely on the lines of the left hand.

# III.   THE FINGERS

What difference does it make if a man's fingers are short or long? All the difference in the world, my dear!

The size, shape and placement of a man's fingers can tell you all sorts of secrets about his character — or lack of it!

This chapter, like the rest of the book, teaches you how to spot hidden character traits. Read it carefully, remembering that the more information you possess, the less likely you are to make a mistake when you choose your next husband or lover.

You should know that if your ideal man is someone who will drop everything to take you on a whimsical picnic to the coast — even though the coast is 300 miles away — you should steer clear of men with strong, long fingers (Fig. 1). Forget about how handsome he is and look at the fingers, because what they can tell you will not disappear the way an attractive face will.

Your long-fingered man will want every part of what began as a fun day planned down to the last pickle. Detail is his bag, and he will leave nothing to chance.

So, leave him quietly planning his details and counting his pickles. In the meantime, be on the look-out for a shorter-fingered companion (Fig. 2) who is probably as whimsical as you are.

This is the man who will be satisfied to enjoy...the wine...the sea...and most importantly impulsive YOU who made him see that a secluded romp in the sand was just what he needed...to hell with the pickles!

Would you have believed that the size of a man's fingers could tell you so much about him? Read on... In addition to denoting an inordinate love of detail, those long fingers reveal tolerance, patience, intellectuality and strong self-control. Those are some pretty heavy qualities, especially if you are the same type of person.

This is a man who takes life seriously. You won't be able to stampede him into making an important decision about your relationship. He takes his time before jumping into anything, including your bed, so don't prod. Let him think the decision is all his.

A thinker, he finds it quite difficult to understand his shorter-fingered brother, who is often impulsive to the point of rashness.

Patience is no virtue to the short-fingered man (Fig. 2). He considers details mundane things, which drudges, like "old long fingers", waste their lives worrying about.

Your short-fingered man, dares to dream the impossible dream, while his counterpart is fully aware of his limitations.

Your impulsive friend also has a penchant for telling others, especially his woman, what to do. If you're indecisive, this is great. If you're not, you could have a few collisions before you can set him straight.

As you can see, the size of your man's fingers can tell you a great deal about him — maybe too much. They can tell you even more once you learn to interpret their spacial relationship to each other.

The space between each finger, as well as the manner in which the fingers are set on the palm, tells you as much or more about your man than the size of his fingers.

Normally set fingers are evenly spaced (Fig. 2). A ruler laid across the base of the fingers would lie in a straight line. Few people achieve this perfection, so if you run across one think twice before letting him get away. Unless of course you have a fetish against perfection!

If any of his fingers are set lower than the others it reduces the major qualities of the mounts, the fleshy pads located at the base of each finger (mounts will be discussed in detail in Chapter 4).

If any finger is set higher than the rest the opposite is true, and the qualities of the mounts are heightened (Fig. 1). The spacial relationship between the thumb and the index finger is also noteworthy.

If your man has a wide space between his thumb and index finger, (Fig. 1) think twice before getting more involved.

This man can give love and give and give and give, but he's rotten when it comes to being on the receiving end. He feels that in accepting your love he becomes obligated to you, and he doesn't want to be obligated to anyone. If you feel having him is worth the emotional investment, remember he is free to move in any direction, and he will, as long as you don't tell him any differently. It's the security of feeling he is free that is important, not the freedom itself.

He's an extrovert, who does everything BIG. If overkill bothers you, stay away; but if 12 carat diamonds are your thing, this may be your man.

When the space between the fingers of Jupiter and Saturn (Fig. 3), the first and second fingers, is wide your man is an independent thinker who will refuse to have his originality stifled by other people's ideas. He'll fight long and hard before he'll change his viewpoint, so why try? The relationship will be much more enjoyable for the two of you if you accept his ideas as part of the man with whom you fell in love.

A wide space between the finger of Saturn and the ring finger (Fig. 3) indicates a happy-go-lucky nature.

This carefree creature likes to do what he likes to do when he wants to do it. Money is simply something to make life worth living — yours and his. He only worries about the green stuff when he doesn't have it. He doesn't even worry about that for long.

Space between the ring finger and the finger of Mercury or little finger (Fig. 3) shows that your man can stand alone. No introvert, he likes people; this fellow simply likes to make his own decisions without any help from the grandstand.

If you're an extrovert looking for another extrovert, the first sign that you've found your match is his hand. If his fingers are all widely spaced (Fig. 3) you know you're on the right track.

The man who can spread his fingers wide apart meets life head on, savoring every precious minute of it. Like you, Ms. Extrovert, he loves to be with people and mixes easily.

Unless you decide to hide your glow under a stuffed shirt, this man will be your friend and maybe more from the minute your eyes make contact.

Beware the man whose fingers can't seem to move

away from each other (Fig. 4). He lacks self-confidence and will prey on yours.

Because this man distrusts himself, he distrusts everyone else. He spends his whole life building walls to keep the rest of the world out.

If you should breach the wall, he'll try to keep you back there with him, removed from all the threatening people who fill his fantasy world.

The man with the tightly clenched hand will also keep a tight fist on the family purse strings. Marry him and be prepared to beg each time you want something frivolous like a new dress or a night on the town.

He is a very serious man with little room for laughter in his life. He will work hard and provide well. If you can wait that long you should be able to live the life of a very merry widow when he's gone.

If the fingers are twisted or crooked in addition to being set closely together, run don't walk to the nearest exit. There is suppressed evil in a hand such as this, and it portends no good for you.

Are you the intellectual type who really doesn't need people? Then find yourself a man whose long thin fingers are close-knit (Fig. 5).

Like you, this man is an introvert, but an intellectual introvert. The two of you should have some interesting conversations behind that brick wall you put up to keep the rest of the world in its place.

Be careful that your analytical introvert's fingers aren't too long, or he'll have no more feeling for you than he has for the rest of the world. The longer the fingers the more likely he will be to find fault with every move you make that is not an attempt to make his self-centered world more comfortable.

Should you choose the intellectual introvert, you may later wish you had chosen the man whose fingers bend backwards. This is the sign of a man who is pleasant and easy going.

Believe it or not, each individual finger tells secrets. Each one will give you more hints about how deeply you should become involved with a specific man.

First you should know that each finger is divided into three phalanges (Fig. 2). The size and location of the phalanges in relationship to the other fingers on his hand is very important.

The first phalange is the nail phalange, and it begins at the tip of the finger. The second is called the middle phalange, because of its location in the middle of the finger. The last phalange ends at the base of the finger.

It is easy for you to determine if your man's fingers are of normal length, and he doesn't need to have any idea what you're up to. Simply give them a careful once-over the next time you caress them. You should both enjoy the examination. You more than he, because you know what you're up to. So enjoy! This is just one more fringe benefit of learning to know your man through hand analysis.

Examine each finger... gently. Does the index finger reach the center of the middle finger's nail phalange (Fig. 3)? If it does match this formula, you're all right. He has a normal-sized finger. Watch out if this finger is longer than normal. Not only does this man want to dominate you and every other women he meets, he has an overweight ego that he'll expect you to feed. Meanwhile you can plan to put your ego into cold storage. He's a taker and giving is fine for somebody else.

He also likes to lead, and you had darn well be ready to follow if you expect to be part of his life. If you like to lead, too, steer clear of this fellow or you could wind up in a first rate collision which could prove fatal to your emotional stability.

If instead you are a masochist at heart, go one step farther and look for the man whose index finger is equal in length to his middle finger (Fig. 1). Tyranny is his long suit, and he should make you blissfully miserable with his unreasonable demands and petty jealousies.

You can expect the barbs to fly if you edge into his limelight. Believe me, this man doesn't care if he hurts you or anyone else who gets in his way.

In addition to all of these other lovely characteristics, this man is also a snob.

If you don't wear the right clothes, know the right people and drink very dry martinis, you don't have very much to worry about in your relationship, because he's going to drop you anyway.

If you're still caressing that hand — and why shouldn't you be? — check out the third finger. Does it reach the middle of the second phalange of the middle finger (Fig. 3) the way a good normal ring finger should?

This finger will tell you if your friend is a gambler. If the finger is the same length as his middle finger you can bet he'll take a chance on anything from a long shot in the Kentucky Derby to you.

Job security is as passe as long-handled johns in Hawaii with his man. Excitement is far more important than prepaid medical insurance and annual salary increases.

He'll climb mountains, shoot rapids, face a charging rhino and even marry more than once — that's the kind of gambler you have on your hands. Life with this man will never be boring, and you might be glad you took a chance — for a short-term affair anyway.

If you insist on an orderly man, drop his hand and him immediately. You both will be happier in the long run — he doesn't need your order any more than you need his constant excitement.

On the other hand, if this chancy guy is your kind of man you'll be pleased to know that he is also likely to be talented and artistic. He needs beauty almost as must as he needs excitement. If you please him as much as he pleases you, expect to always be surrounded by beautiful things.

Take his middle finger, touching it gently while you look at it. See how easy, if a trifle devious, this is?

If the finger is short with smooth joints, you'd better cut out the teasing — even if you are only doing it for scientific research!

This type of middle finger is indicitive of animalistic desires that are a bit more than you may be ready to handle. In addition, it hides a morbid nature and gross irresponsibilities, an unattractive combination at best.

Having a long middle finger isn't much better. This man is a contradiction in extremes. He tends to jump from fiery passion to frigidity in one easy bound.

Idealogically, he also tends to be a fanatic. Unless your social, religious an political beliefs are quite similar — look out! You'll either wind up not speaking to each other, or as his personal punching bag.

We're nearing the end of our examination — the little finger. Believe me, it can tell you more than a little about the men in your life. (Fig. 4)

If this miniature finger is longer than average, it denotes an eloquent person — one who will be able to think of hundreds of ways to say, "I love you." Nothing wrong with that!

If this finger is crooked in addition to being long, his eloquence and his diplomacy may go several steps beyond the truth. "Love" is just another word in his large vocabulary. Like the others, it is merely a tool to get what he desires.

The finger also tends to take the characteristics of the Mount of Mercury, which is discussed in depth in Chapter 4.

If you haven't let go of his hand — and why should you? — check out his nails (Fig. 7). You may find a little dirt if he isn't too fastidious, but you will also find revelations about his disposition, health, character and temper under those semi-flexible pieces of protein.

Short nails show energy, a hypercritical nature, a short fuse and a total lack of patience. This man is also curious, but it's a curiosity that too often leads him into argument.

Long nails are indicitive of a more quiet nature. This man may lack some of his counterpart's energy, but he will also be more patient and understanding of your shortcomings.

The color of his nails can also help identify some unhealthy character traits. If you man is healthy and has very white nails, he is likely to be cold and icy. Every word, every movement will be deliberate as he conserves his limited energy.

Passion or a lack of it is clearly shown in the color of the nails. The redder the nails, the more deep and intense are your man's inner fires. It's up to you to decide if you want to be the fireman, who stokes those inner flames.

You will have to take the bitter with the sweet, because a violent temper comes packaged with all that passion. Can you control both those blazes? That's a decision you'll have to make on your own.

His fingers have revealed all sorts of hidden information about his character — information that can greatly affect both your lives.

Remember that the fingers are only one part, though a very integral part, of hand analysis. What you have gleaned from this chapter cannot stand alone. It must be looked at in conjunction with the entire book.

It is important that you understand the individual parts of the hand, before you can expect to master it in its entirety.

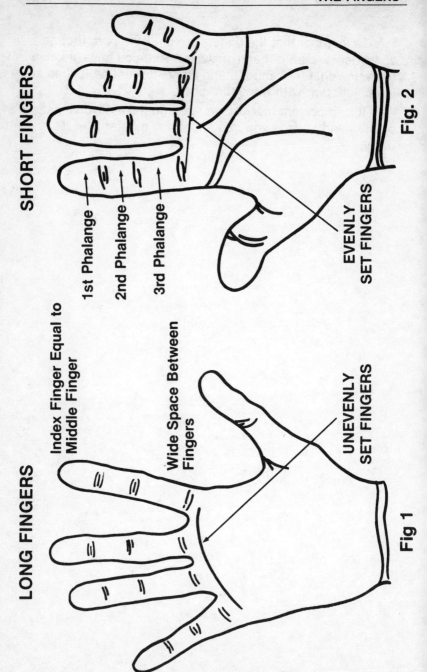

## SHORT FINGERS

1st Phalange

2nd Phalange

3rd Phalange

EVENLY SET FINGERS

Fig. 2

## LONG FINGERS

Index Finger Equal to Middle Finger

Wide Space Between Fingers

UNEVENLY SET FINGERS

Fig 1

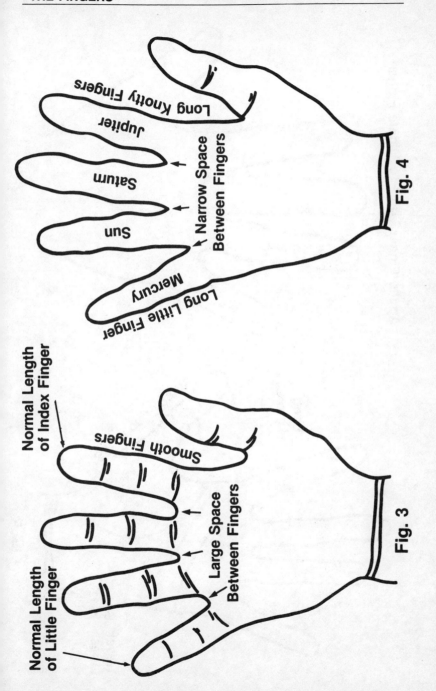

Normal Length of Index Finger

Smooth Fingers

Large Space Between Fingers

Normal Length of Little Finger

Fig. 3

Long Knotty Fingers

Jupiter

Saturn

Sun

Narrow Space Between Fingers

Mercury

Long Little Finger

Fig. 4

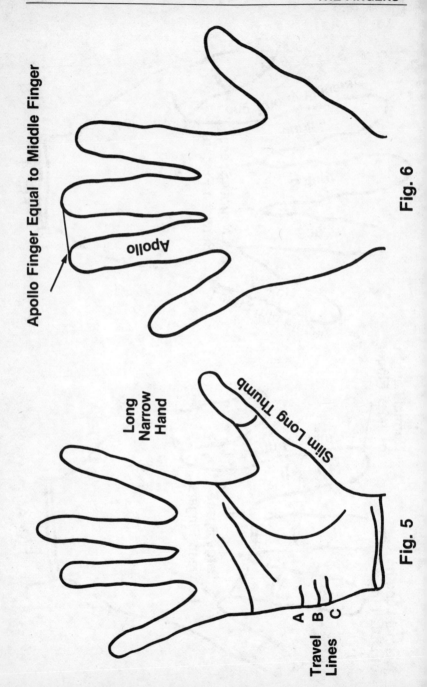

Apollo Finger Equal to Middle Finger

Apollo

**Fig. 6**

Long Narrow Hand

Slim Long Thumb

Travel Lines

A
B
C

**Fig. 5**

# TYPES OF NAILS

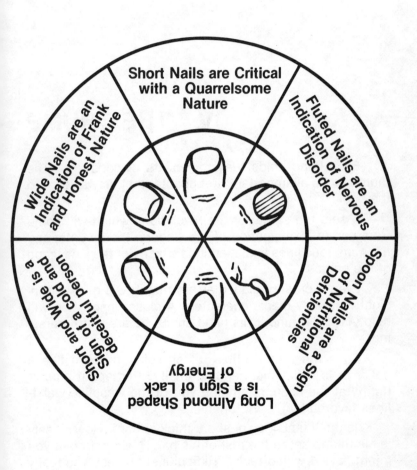

**Fig. 7**

# IV.  THE THUMB

Each hand holds the story of its owner's life.  The thumb is the all important first chapter that draws you into the book.

It sets the stage for the revelations which will come from careful examination of the fingers, the mounts, and the numerous lines and m arkings which dot the landscape of the palm.

Even a cursory glance at his thumb will give you insights into any man's character.  A closer inspection will help you determine if his hand and/or he are worth pursuing.

Does the thumb stick out straight and hard like a poker or is it flexible, bending easily? Perhaps it nips in tightly at the base, reminding you of the wasplike waistlines favored by the Victorians.

Is the thumb long or short, thick or thin?  How closely is his thumb set to the rest of his hand?  Unimportant you might say!  I would reply, "Ridiculous!" unless you really have no interest in the man whose hand you will be scrutinizing closely in the very near future.

The larger your man's thumb (Fig. 1-B) the more likely he will act based on reason, rather than emotions.  This man is strong and forceful. He's a natural leader who would love to lead you - - possibly to the altar, but just as possibly down the garden path.

If you enjoy playing follow the leader and can do it reasonably well, don't hesitate to chase after your large-thumbed fellow.

Don't shed any tears later, if you find yourself rebelling against this self-styled monarch. Remember you chose to stay with him in spite of what his thumb said.

Do you prefer a man who is ruled by the heart rather than the head? Then hope your man has a small thumb (Fig. 1-A), a sign of a romantic. Not only is he romantic, he is easily led and almost as easily dominated. This could be an added bonus if you have a large, forceful thumb.

Expect to be continually bathed in love by your small-thumbed man, unless of course you force him into someone else's tub by not returning his love.

He'll read you poetry by the hour, stroke your hair gently by firelight and write you letters that will bring warmth to your face for years to come.

A large or small thumb does not tell you everything. You have to look at it more closely, breaking it into its individual parts — not literally! Please. . .

The thumb, like the fingers, is divided into three parts or phalanges. These phalanges, beginning at the top of the thumb, illustrate will power, logic and his ability to share love (Fig. 1-C).

It is only logical that the large thumbed man is more likely to offer a balance of these qualities than the small thumbed man. Balance is really the name of the man-hunting game, isn't it?

After all, who wants a hopelessly incurable romantic for keeps-except another hopeless romantic? He's just as likely to fall head over heels in love with your best friend—

while professing undying love to you. And all in the same week!

By the same token, who wants a man who has such a strong will power that he successfully resists all of your temptations? Being able to say "Get thee behind me Satan" is one thing, but being able to push you into the background while he goes over some silly account, is quite another.

If you want to know how easy it will be for him to resist you at your most irresistable, look closely at his nail phalange --the one at the top. The larger the phalange in relationship to the middle phalange, the stronger his will power will be.

If your man has a larger than normal nail phalange, he will be able to say 'no' for a very long time. On the other hand, he will be quite willing to persist until you say, "Yes."

When this top phalange is small, your man will be unable to resist temptation. It won't matter if the temptress is a blond, brunette or redhead. More than once the temptation may turn out to be a bottle instead of another woman. It really doesn't matter what the tempter is, this man won't have the will power to resist.

The middle phalange shows logic. It begins at the joint in the thumb and ends at the base (Fig. 1-C).

You really don't want this phalange to overshadow the nail phalange (Fig. 1-B). After all, the best and most logical ideas in the world are useless if you lack the will power to carry them out.

The man with the large second phalange, is more likely to see someone else steal the ideas he formulates and put them into action. You'll quickly tire of being wife or mistress to a first-rate second banana, constantly seeing someone else get the praise that should be his. You're smart enough to realize that whatever glories he gains spill over to the woman he loves.

The best possible combination is a first phalange that is slightly larger, but not much, than the second. This provides balance. If you also desire success in a man, make sure he has a thumb that is larger than average, too.

We mustn't forget the man whose thumb nips in like a woman's waistline (fig. 2-A). This is the sign of a tactful man, one who will go out of his way to keep from hurting your feelings.

He is also refined, and coarseness on your part will not be tolerated for long. So do as he does, if you want to remain in the picture for long.

This man is a lot of things, but a handy man isn't one of them. One of the reasons you have money is so you can hire someone more crass to do disagreeable chores, according to him. Meanwhile he'll accept more responsible work, like being chairman of the board.

In addition to size, you should determine what type of thumbs the men in your life have, then choose the type that best fits into your lifestyle.

There are two basic types of thumbs — the supple or flexible thumb (Fig. 1-A) and the straight-rigid thumb (Fig. 1-B). Both types have their strong points. Everything depends on what you are looking for in a man.

The flexible thumb shows just that, flexibility. This man can adapt to almost any situation. He will move easily from one woman to another, as long as it fits his needs.

Extravagance is another characteristic of the supple thumbed man. He pours out everything — love, money and time — with no thought to the future. It's a simple case of enjoying this man today without banking on the future. If you decide to tie yourself to him permanently, make sure that you are flexible, too.

Remember you'll be tying yourself to a man with a childlike concept of morals. He won't understand why you can't understand why he does things he's sure to do. After all, it's perfectly reasonable to him. If you can adapt, fine. If you can't accept him like he is, leave. No matter what he says, he'll never change.

If you can give up imagination and creativity in your love making in exchange for stability and endurance, try to capture a stiff-thumbed fellow. His thumb automatically tells you that he is a far more practical man than the man with the flexible thumb.

He's a meat and potatoes, no-nonsense sort of guy who, very likely, will plod his way to success. While he may not be overly imaginative in his love making, he'll be true, which may be far more important to you.

Look for him to exercise caution, whether making business transactions or choosing a wife. This man doesn't rush into anything, and maybe that's why people see him as a success — if not much fun.

He won't be demonstrative in or out of the public light. He proves his love by providing you with an adequate bank account now, and a substantial insurance policy for later. There will always be food on the table and clothes in the closet if you get this man committed to you.

The rigid-thumbed man may surprise you if his third phalange, which is basically the Mount of Venus (Fig. 1-E), is well developed. This mount, beginning at the base of the thumb and ending at the base of the palm, determines sensuality. If it is well developed, the passion is there despite the austerity of the rest of the thumb.

As I will say over and over, you have to look at the entire hand before making any final decisions about whether a specific man is or is not for you. One bad point in the thumb can easily be offset — or strengthened — by the mounts or a specific line. Carefully study the hand in its entirety, beginning but not ending with the individual parts.

We still aren't finished with this important part, since the thumb is the key that unlocks many doors of the hand. How a man's thumb sets on his hand is especially important to you.

Is his thumb high? Then it is also probably rigid. This doesn't necessarily mean he's a rigid "right-thinking" man, but it's a real possibility.

When the high-set thumb is rigid (Fig. 1-B), and the fingers are rigid, know when to stop. Stubbornness is this man's forte, and it will be impossible to beat him at his game. Learn how to give in gracefully, and you'll be the winner in the long run.

If his whole hand is rigid, he's very self-conscious. Build up his self-image, and you'll win yourself a permanent niche in his heart if not in his life. Help draw him out of his shyness gently, don't shove him into the limelight.

Does his thumb set low on his hand (Fig. 1-C)? If it does, prepare to give him lots of room to run, because he's an independent cuss. If you not only promise, but, in fact, give him his freedom, he will be more than generous with you.

Examine his thumb carefully. Note the set...the size...the phalanges... as you inspect that all important member, try to recall all you have learned about different thumb types.

Write down what you find. Do it now, if he knows what you're up to — later, if he doesn't. It's almost time to progress to the study of his fingers.

If you're distressed over what you did or didn't find in his thumb, remember that the fingers, mounts and various lines in the head can modify what his thumb told you about him.

Too, don't expect to be perfect on your first attempt. Remember practice makes perfect. Inspect several hands before you do Mr. Right's. In addition to being educational and giving you the experience you need — it could be fun.

## TYPES OF THUMBS

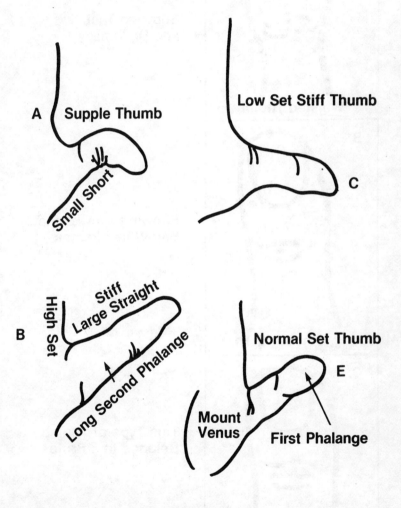

**Fig. 1**

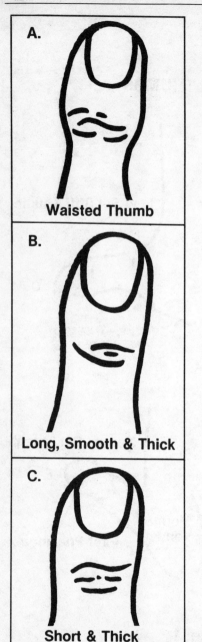

**A.**

**Waisted Thumb**

**B.**

**Long, Smooth & Thick**

**C.**

**Short & Thick**

# TYPES OF THUMBS

**Showing Tact
and Diplomacy**

**Showing An Obstinate
Self-Willed Person**

**This Type of Thumb
Belongs to a Brute**

**Fig. 2**

# V. THE MOUNTS

Seven pads of muscle located at the base of the fingers and along the outside of the palm are the strongest indicators of your man's virtues and vices.

These fleshy pads are the Mounts of Jupiter, Saturn, Sun, Mercury, Moon, Venus and Upper and Lower Mars (Fig. 1).

It is easy to see the more pronounced mounts. If you want to become more familiar with each mount, the best way is through touch — and what man would mind your touch?

The more pronounced a mount is, the more your man possesses the characteristics attributed to the mount. Accordingly, the less pronounced the mount, the more its special properties are watered-down.

Occasionally you will run across a hand that is devoid of mounts, though you may have to touch a lot of hands before finding a mountless one. More often one, two or three mounts are developed with one mount dominating the others.

The best hand to look for, according to most hand analysts, is one where all the mounts are equally developed. This hand shows a well balanced man who has it all together. It is also as rare as the mountless hand, showing that well-balanced men aren't as common as most men believe. However, women have known that all along!

MOUNT OF JUPITER — does your man like power and lean strongly towards a military, political or religious career? If your answer is yes, he more than likely has a strongly developed Mount of Jupiter (Fig. 1).

To determine if this is true, look at the fleshy pad located at the base of the index finger or Finger of Jupiter. If the mount is higher and larger than the other mounts on his hands, you have a Jupiterian in your hands.

This man, as you well know if you know him at all, is a contradiction of ambition and idealism. The Jupiterian is one of the few people who can make the two hang together for the betterment of everyone, including himself.

He loves the public spotlight. If you meet his standards and can stand the glare he'll let you bask in its warmth with him. Remember, if you want to stay with this man, you can't ever stand still, or you'll find youself standing alone.

Life with the Jupiterian is a constant adventure. He is constantly searching for new knowledge in tempting forbidden areas like the occult. Nothing is too bizarre for him.

Friends, fortune and love will come easily to this man. You will always have to be on guard against female vandals, who would like to sack and pillage your relationship. You really can't blame them, so be sure that you hold him tightly and often, If you don't, someone else will.

Cover him with your warmth like a loose blanket. give him the security of your love without strangling him, and he'll never feel the need to try another bed.

Sex is very important to the Jupiterian, but the right woman can provide all of the variety he needs. This man takes his love seriously, and if you treat him right, he will have no desire for an outside fling.

Expect to be placed on a pedestal by this man; after all, he chose you and he's perfect. Once you're on the pedestal don't slip. If you do decide to edge away from the home fires, do it with the full understanding that a Jupiterian does not forgive and forget. Once he becomes disillusioned, he is like all the king's men with Humpty Dumpty; he can't put the illusions back together again.

Occasionally you will have to act as a buffer for your Jupiterian. One of his greatest faults is his brutal frankness. You may have to soften some of the blows his tongue delivers so easily.

Just as his magnetic personality draws many friends to him, his uncurbed mouth makes him many enemies. It will be your job to act as peacemaker, especially with people who are important to his career.

You will be able to count on his being a success in any field if he has both a long headline and a long thumb.

A Jupiterian tends to overdo almost everything, especially in his later years. Again, it will be up to you to protect him from himself.

Look out for his tendencies to overeat and drink to excess. You may find yourself guarding both the pantry and the liquor cabinet. If those doors are kept locked, make sure the one to the bedroom is left wide open. That kind of compensation beats a ham sandwich any day of the week.

MOUNT OF SATURN — This mount, which shows intellectual ability, is located at the base of the middle finger, or Finger of Saturn (Fig. 1).

The man whose Mount of Saturn is the most highly developed of all his mounts is indeed a deep thinker, but it is rare for him to occupy himself with pleasant thoughts.

This man is a pessimist who ultimately will vent his

cynicism on you. He'll always find it unbelievable that someone as great as you could really love someone like himself.

He'll constantly be searching for proof that you're having an affair with someone else. If his jealousies reach the extremes he's capable of, you probably will fulfill his fantasies. Why not?

He is tight with both his money and his affections. If there is still something about him that makes you jump into the fire regardless of the warning in the mount, be prepared to spend your life on a budget — physically and financially.

Don't be surprised later to find your Saturnarian feels the best company in the world is himself. Be prepared to go searching for a good "friend" away from home.

When you are with this man, expect to cope with frequent changes in mood and deep depressions.

Does sex rank highly on your list of pleasures? Plan to find it with someone other than your moody Saturnarian. He is just as eratic in the erotic department as he is in the rest of his life.


MOUNT OF SUN — Ah, if this mount, the Mount of Sun, is the dominant mount, you're in luck — unless, of course, you insist on lasting relationships!

The mount, located under the ring finger (Fig. 1), reveals a cheerful, optimistic personality when it is well developed. People are immediately drawn to this man, and he to them.

The problem lies in that he is always being drawn to new people. Remember, he can't help himself, so accept and enjoy while the interest is fresh. Don't expect him to become a permanent fixture, even if you marry him.

He's a delight in bed, and the memories should be worth whatever pain is left when he moves on. You can keep those fires burning a little longer by remembering little things like your appointment with the hairdresser.

Appearances are especially important to the Sun Man. He wants both his temporary home and his temporary woman to be as attractive as possible. Forget this and you may find him looking for replacements sooner than you desire.

It's quite possible your Sun Man is an artist. If he isn't, he has the artist's love and perception of beauty.

His interest in the arts will lead the two of you to spend your leisure hours with other creative people.

MOUNT OF MERCURY — If your man's Mount of Mercury is well developed, you can expect to have a large bank account and more than your share of loneliness. Of course you can always compensate elsewhere.

The mount, located beneath the little finger, shows a man devoted to his family image, his community and his business.

The Mercurian, when he has a well developed mount and a long little finger, is a good manager of both time and people. He is shrewd in his business dealings. Don't expect him to recite his financial coups to you, because after all, you're only a woman. The Mercurian male will never let you forget the female's inferiority.

He appears to be devoted to you and the children, if you are married. This is the surface show of a man who is rarely home. His time is more evenly divided between business associates and community projects. His lack of real devotion is a secret you're supposed to help keep in return for a healthy bank account.

A realist, he understands people and knows how to use their weaknesses to his advantage. He is such a strong person that it is easy for him to influence others.

The Mercurian has both a public and private face in

business, too. He is always polite and attentive to his clients, but his employees see a different man. There is a definite lack of mutual respect at the office.

When the Mercurian decides to settle down, he looks for a woman who is intelligent, budget conscious, community-minded and OBEDIENT.

He desires a woman who can handle any emergency that may arise at home since he is rarely there. He also wants an unblemished wife, so hide those past affairs if you really want this man. There are, after all, times when honesty is not the best policy!

Once you are safely established in his home, don't transgress. If you do, make sure that you don't get caught. Forgiveness is not one of his virtues.

If you are not already married to this man, think twice about tying yourself to him if you have strong sexual desires. He'll either destroy you through sexual repression, or drive you into the arms of other men who will be more than willing to give you what your frustrated, sexually-inhibited Mercurian cannot.

If the Mount of Mercury is strong and the Finger of Mercury is very crooked you have another kind of problem. This man will scheme and lie his way in and out of your life. Have fun with him briefly, but don't trust him with anything more important than a few hours of physical pleasure.

MOUNT OF THE MOON — Does the pioneer spirit exist deep within you waiting for release? Do names of places such as Lisbon, Buenos Aires, Paris, Zurich and Berlin call up irresistible longings and visions? Then you are the kind of free spirit who will delight a man with a very highly developed Mount of the Moon (Fig. 1). He will delight you, too — in the beginning.

He'll sweep you off your feet with unwavering attention, until he has conquered you. Once the initial battle is won he is very likely to decide to forego the rest of the war.

In the beginning stages of the war he'll be willing to accompany you to any and all the glittering capitals of the world, which he'll promptly lay at your feet.

He rarely prizes his real life coups, preferring to desert them for the delightful nymphs who inhabit his fantasy world.

The real thing, unfortunately for you, never quite lives up to his sexual fantasies. Once he has conquered you he will sink deeper and deeper into the unreal world he has created, and it will be impossible for you to entice him back to reality.

Your Lunarian is self-indulgent. A purely sensual man, he enjoys giving in to everything that pleases his senses. This will include booze, broads and erotic fantasies. Nothing short of the grave will provide him with complete relief from his own feeling of sexual inadequacy.

He will follow a pattern moving from butterfly to butterfly. Occasionally he will go so far as to marry, when it fits his battle plan.

If you agree to play his game knowing full well what his hands tell you, don't complain when the cold, lonely nights begin. Be prepared to substitute a hot water bottle and your own fantasies for the man you need.

The Lunarian lacks self-confidence, one of the reasons he resorts to fantasy stimulation, but he does have talents. An artistic person by nature, his talent may be carefully preserved in a bundle of love letters or poems he dedicated to you when the hunt began.

He is a weak person, and a Cancer with a strong mothering personality may be the perfect mate for him. She can give and give and give, while demanding very little for herself.

Don't be surprised if he spends every cent on his own self-indulgences. Travel is his greatest weakness. He is not content with reading about the rest of the world. He has to see it and feel it beneath him — like a woman to be conquered and then left.

Life will not be easy with this hypersensitive, emotional, and suspicious creature, but neither will it be boring if you can fill his mother role. There will always be another man around to fulfill your sexual needs.

There are two Mounts of Mars. The Lower Mount of Mars is located on the edge of the palm below the Mount of Mercury. The Upper Mount of Mars is located beneath the Mount of Jupiter.

If either of these mounts is developed you have a fighter on your hands. A well developed Mount of Upper Mars reveals a fighting spirit — an idealist. This man has strong moral character, and can easily resist temptations you may throw in front of him because of his strong self-control.

If the mount is underdeveloped, the opposite is true. This man is a dissolute character who gives in to every desire.

When the Lower Mount of Mars is well developed, your man just plain likes to fight, so keep plenty of bandages in the house and don't forget to pay the medical insurance premiums.

He can be courageous, saving a damsel in distress, or petty, fighting over an imagined slight. One thing is in his favor — if he decides to fight, he usually has the necessary physical strength to win.

When the lower mount is underdeveloped, your friend is more likely to be sensitive and a bit of a coward. That means don't push him into positions where he will be forced to defend your honor. You might not like what you see, and he may no longer want you for the embarrassment you have caused.

MOUNT OF VENUS — Now we come to the mount for you girls who consider physical satisfaction the number one thing in your life — the Mount of Venus.

This mount, located at the base of the thumb (Fig. 1), is the best indicator of your man's sexual desires — or the lack of those desires.

If the mount is large, high and firm it is a sign of vitality, love and stored-up passion. His sexual feelings are strong and close to the surface, easy for you to arouse.

When the mount is large, high and soft, most of the same qualities are present, but this man lacks the vitality that goes with a firmer Mount of Venus.

If your sexual appetite is large, drop the man with the small flat Mount of Venus — he can't do a thing for you. He is cold, and his inability to produce in the bedroom makes him fickle. According to him any signs of impotence are your fault, not his — but we know better, don't we?

It is very important to choose a man with the same type of Mount of Venus for a marriage partner or lover. Otherwise one of you will never be satisfied.

The real tiger is the man with the high, firm, well-developed Mount of Venus that is crossed by many fine lines and slightly reddish in color. Sexual experimentation is this man's bag, and he is open to any suggestion — the more daring, the better.

Because he likes variety, he is far more likely to stray away from the home fires. That's one of the chances you take with this fellow. If you have a similar mount, you'll be ready to change partners, too.

See what you have learned about your favorite man just by looking and hopefully caressing seven small pads of muscle on his palms?

I hope you didn't find anything you didn't want to find, but isn't it better to be forewarned about character faults, than to learn about them after it's too late?

THE MOUNTS

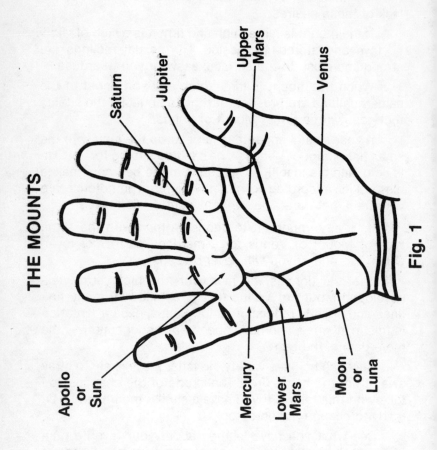

Fig. 1

Saturn

Jupiter

Upper Mars

Venus

Apollo or Sun

Mercury

Lower Mars

Moon or Luna

# VI.  MARKS AND LINES

"Reality is stranger than fiction" certainly holds true in hand analysis, probably more so than in any other science. The effect a tiny mark, such as a star of island, can have on a man's life is often unbelievable.

The cause and effect relationship that results from the various marks that are found on the hand is very real. The worst thing you could do during your hand stroking investigation is to ignore these symbols when you find them dotting his palm.

Almost every mark can be looked upon as a defect — often a defect that could mar your relationship. This is especially true of islands, breaks, tassels and chained formations. They usually have a negative effect on the individual line they touch. The effect each has on a specific line will be discussed in the chapter on that line.

Let's look at breaks first (Fig. 1). A break is a clear separation of the main line. If the break is very tiny, the forces which follow through the body can often jump the break with little ill effect.

These forces cannot bridge a large gap. They stop for the duration of the break, which you can figure out by the chronological chart of the line the break affects.

The breaks often have built-in repairs. Check out the area surrounding the breaks, as carefully as the breaks themselves. Occasionally the breaks have overlapping lines (Fig. 2). These overlaps either halt or soften the damage caused by the separation.

A sister line (Fig. 3), is a fine line running alongside the main line, and it also heals the break.

Another healer and a positive sign is the square (Fig. 4). The boxlike symbol protects your man from the bad effect of any negative mark it covers, including a break.

Every water pilot knows the problems islands (Fig. 5) can cause. They are just as dangerous when found on your man's palm.

An island is a definite defect, which can be offset by a square. It does diminish the line it sets on. Again the chronological chart on the specific line affected will tell you when the bad luck will hit and approximately when it will go away.

The effects of the island as well as the other marks last for a definite period of time — not forever.

A grill is another serious defect. (Fig. 6). The grill is a series of fine lines crisscrossing each other in a squarelike pattern.

If he has stars on his hands (Fig. 7) as well as in his eyes you can look for a variety of meanings. Unlike the other marks a star can indicate success or failure — it depend on where the star is located.

It's a good sign on either the Mount of Jupiter, the Sun Mount or the Sun Line. If you find a star anywhere else, watch out for ill effects.

A star on the Mount of Jupiter means that honors have or will be heaped on your man. If the star shines on the Mount of Apollo, and if he also has a star on the Sun Line, he will have public success. In this case, a double beats a single any day.

Everyone has a cross to bear at one time or another in his life, and often those crosses are in his hand (Fig. 8). If you man is lucky, his cross will be surrounded by the protective square.

Lines should be straight and clear. Weak wavy lines do nothing for a man, except weaken the qualities of that particular line.

A line will often terminate in a fork or a tassel (Fig. 9). If you have a choice of one or the other, take the man whose lines end in forks, instead of the one with the tasseled line. This holds true for every line except the life line, where even a fork is dangerous instead of strengthening.

Tassels are always debilitating. They drain the power from the line, whirling it into nothingness.

Branches can work with or against your friend (Fig. 10). If they reach upward they accentuate the power of the line. Downward moving branches have the opposite draining effect.

Another sign is the triangle. If you're an intellectual and are looking for suitable companionship, look for a man with this sign on his palm. He should be your match.

Look at many hands and learn to recognize these marks. Now you know what they are and the kinds of effects they can have on your life through your choice of a playmate.

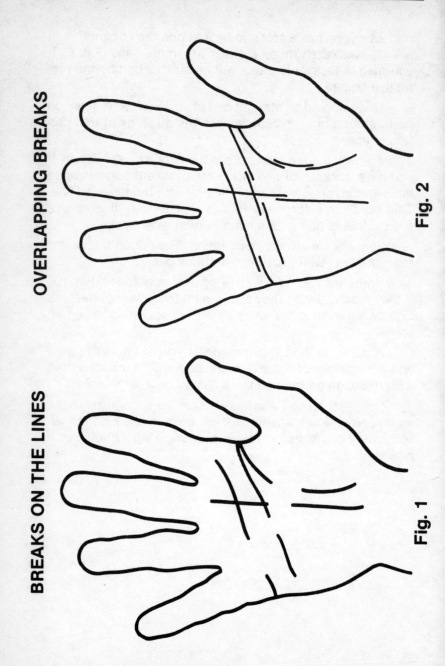

**BREAKS ON THE LINES**

Fig. 1

**OVERLAPPING BREAKS**

Fig. 2

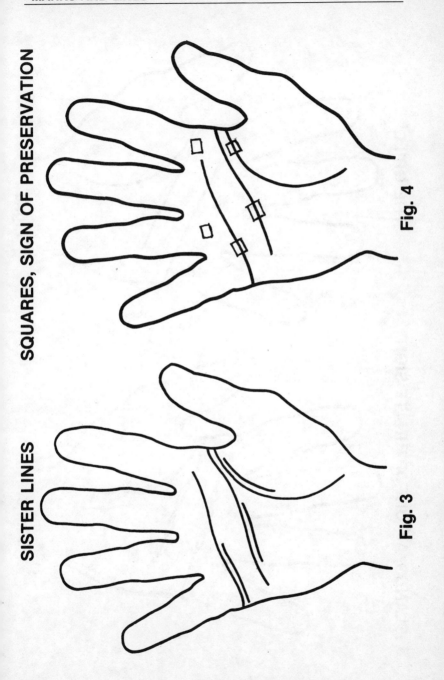

SISTER LINES

SQUARES, SIGN OF PRESERVATION

Fig. 3

Fig. 4

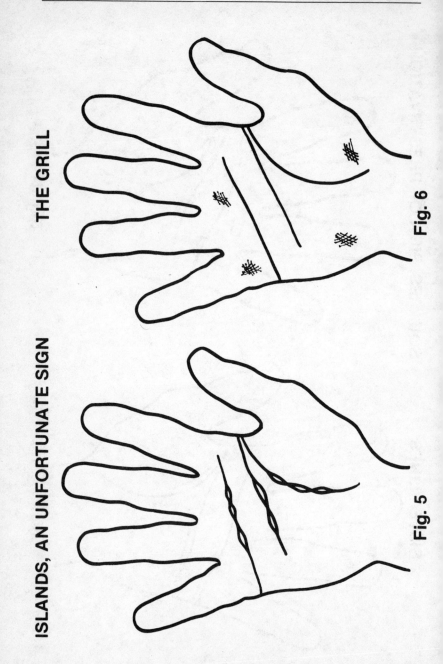

THE GRILL

Fig. 6

ISLANDS, AN UNFORTUNATE SIGN

Fig. 5

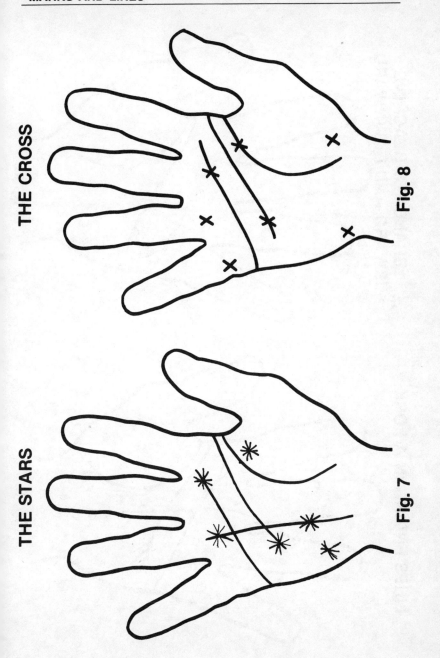

THE CROSS

THE STARS

Fig. 8

Fig. 7

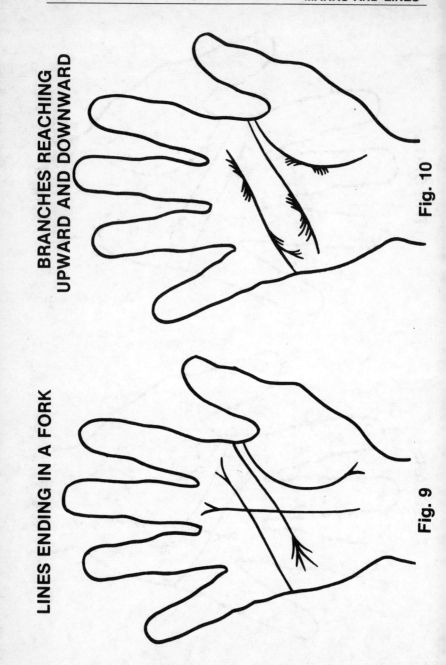

LINES ENDING IN A FORK

BRANCHES REACHING
UPWARD AND DOWNWARD

Fig. 9

Fig. 10

# TRIANGLE IS A LUCKY SIGN

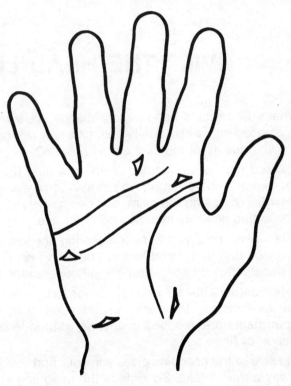

**Fig. 11**

# VII. THE HEAD LINE

What's in a man's head is very clearly shown in his hand. The head line, or mentality line, carefully defines the quantity and quality of his intellectual powers.

Located near or connected to the life line, the head line moves horizontally across the palm. When there is only one major line crossing the palm, one can safely assume it is the head line and this man has no heart line.

This line is perhaps the most revealing line in a man's hand, so look carefully. In addition to outlining your man's mental capabilities it shows how he will cope under strain.

Split personalities, mental disorders, anxieties, suicidal tendencies, traumatic experiences and major disappointments are exposed to anyone who understands the science of hand analysis.

The size of the head line gives you your first indication of the way a man thinks. So look, is the head line long or short? Is it deep or shallow?

When the line is short (Fig. 1) it is indicative of limited intellectual capacity. You can expect this man to enjoy your body more than your brains, but what's wrong with that!

The longer the line, the more thoughtful and reflective

the man is. If he can combine his reflective ability with a strong sense of will, you both have a winning combination.

Normally the head line is connected to the life line (Fig. 2). The connection between these lines lets you know if he can think for himself. Many men can't, you know.

It is at the point of separation of the head line and life line that a man begins to assert himself and make his own decisions.

If there is no connection between these two lines (Fig. 3), you have a man who has never relied on anyone else since the day his mother changed his last diaper.

This man sticks up for himself. If you're his cup of tea, he'll fight your battles, too. A natural leader, he will always fight his way to the top of the pack, usually without causing too much bitterness to the rest of the pack.

The man with the independent head line is blessed with foresight. His decisions, based on long range planning, will astound his associates. They'll swear he's psychic because of his uncanny accurateness in calculating future turns of events. Maybe he is, but you'll never convince this man.

He will be bold and daring in both his public and private lives. While he dominates others in a pleasant manner, he does not like to be dominated. This means keeping a loose rein, while you use your best hidden persuaders to nudge him in the direction you're heading.

A separation between his head and life lines is good, but you can have too much of a good thing. If the gap is too wide (Fig. 4), his independence can turn into recklessness.

If his head line is short in addition to being widely separated from his life line, you are playing with fire. His total disregard for rules could get you both in a lot of trouble.

Once you're in trouble look for him to think of himself first. He's number one, and he won't ever let you forget it.

A long head line that slopes towards the Mount of the Moon (Fig. 5) points towards a more creative and imaginitive man. He knows lots of fun games, and if you're nice to him, he'll let you play.

Be careful about the games you play with this man if the head line extends deeply into the Lunar Mount (Fig. 6). Often, this man is unable to separate fact from fiction, and the game can get rough.

Whether he paints, writes or has musical talent isn't important. He may or he may not, but he definitely has an appreciation for beauty and its creators.

Are you one of those people who love to cry at maudlin movies and weep sad songs? Find a man whose head line curves towards the Mount of the Moon, and who has a well developed Mount of Saturn (Fig. 7). This man suffers from depression — don't we all — and if he's creative the end result could be a sad story or musical composition.

At least he reaps something from the hours he spends feeling sorry for himself besides anxiety pangs. If you're the cause of his depression, he may even dedicate a sonnet to you.

You can expect anything except laughter from this Sad Sack. If he truly is creative, his talent may make up for the near permanent doldrums he sinks himself into. Maybe, but don't bet on it.

Does his head line curve up towards the Mount of Mercury (Fig. 8) after following a long straight path across his palm? This points towards a successful career in business or public life. Take your pick, then guide him in the direction you think is best for you both. Nothing like being the woman behind a successful man!

Another successful head line is the one that branches to the Mount of Mercury (Fig. 9). This man will embrace success even more strongly than he embraces you. He doesn't just like money and the power it buys, he loves it. Don't you? Remember, as long as you have him, both the money and the power automatically belong to you, too.

He is a fellow with a gambling streak. He'll do almost anything for a quick buck, and his glib tongue is one of his greatest assets.

Watch out for that silvery tongue! It has been the undoing of many a sweet young thing, and you're not immune. Then, maybe you're not looking for immunity. While this man can never be accused of being "Mr. Clean", at the same time no one can accuse him of being boring.

Does his head line send off a branch towards the Mount of Jupiter (Fig. 10)? This man, too, wants to be rich. If his ambition is coupled with will power, nothing can stop him and you.

This man needs help. All you have to do to keep him happy is pour the right mix of fuel to his enlarged ego. Oh, yes, keep yourself physically and mentally fit to cope with your upward mobility. If you can't hack it in the circles he plans to move in,you're on your way out, Baby! An expensive dress shop, good hairdresser and frequent trips to galleries and libraries can keep you in there fighting.

Another important branch to the head line is the one that shoots off towards the Mount of the Sun (Fig. 11). People will gravitate towards this man, liking him instantly. Some of the female types may like him too much, so be on the lookout for predators.

This line is one I have seen frequently in the hands of social leaders, artists and musicians. They love the limelight, but unlike some types, they like to share the glow they move about in. If this sign shows up in your man's hand expect to spend many evenings with others as talented and charming as he is.

An interesting thing happens when the head line sends an off shoot to the heart line (Fig. 12). By determining the age of the man at the time the branch was formed you can also determine the date his intellect began to control his emotions.

There are reasons for the advent of ice ages in people just as there are for continents. The line is in all probability the result of an unpleasant liaison. A girl friend or a wife really socked it to the poor guy, and being a man, he's carried his distrust to anything that wears skirts.

Therefore, expect this man to put any decisions concerning your relationship out of the realm of the emotions. He'll rate you on a scale of ten, which was devised through pure logic — to hell with depending on electricity and body chemistry!

So much for him...when your man's head line ends in a fork (Fig. 13) you've found yourself a wise and tolerant man. Not perfect himself, he can understand and accept your little weaknesses.

Soloman-like, he will explore any situation carefully. This means he will look at all sides before passing judgement. If you're in the wrong, he'll let you know it, because love doesn't make this man blind.

Hope that as you look at his hand you don't find any islands (Fig. 14) breaking up the head line. They usually mean that he is having difficulty coping with his life.

Coping won't become any easier until the islands float away to wherever islands go, when they leave the hand. The interim period will be fraught with emotional turmoil. It takes a big woman to stay and help her man work out his problems. Stay, if you like, but no one would blame you for copping out.

If you decide to stick it out with your man, you can very likely find out what is causing the problems by looking at the other lines in his hand. Cause and effect are written very plainly in everyone's hands.

For example do you see a head line starting from the Mount of Jupiter (Fig. 15)? If shouldn't surprise you that this man leads easily. This is his gift — the ability to influence, manipulate and guide people in any group he joins.

Luckily his leadership abilities are tempered with tact. Otherwise he might lead you down the road to disaster. This man is as reliable as your father, though more fun and certainly more desirable.

The longer the headline, the more intellectual this man is, so you can't be any dummy if he's interested enough to let you check out his hand.

Better yet is the man whose head line begins under the Mount of Jupiter and then connects to the life line (Fig. 16). This is the best possible line, especially if it is long and clear and stretches across the palm. This man can and will achieve any goal he sets for himself.

If fighting definitely isn't your cup of tea, steer clear of the man with a head line beginning inside the life line from the Mount of Mars (Fig. 17). Life with him will be one battle after another, and you'll lose everyone, and possibly a tooth or two to boot.

He will argue over whether it's day or night. Who needs that kind of life? Besides, we women occasionally like to get in the last word! You never will with this man.

Just when you think you have him psyched out on an issue, he'll change his viewpoint. Don't tell him that! He'll never believe you.

He doesn't even have a sense of humor to balance all his bad character traits. You'll need one if you decide to go ahead with this man.

The head line, as you have seen, is another indicator of a man's intellect and emotional stability. Primarily it tells you if he thinks, and what he's most likely to think about.

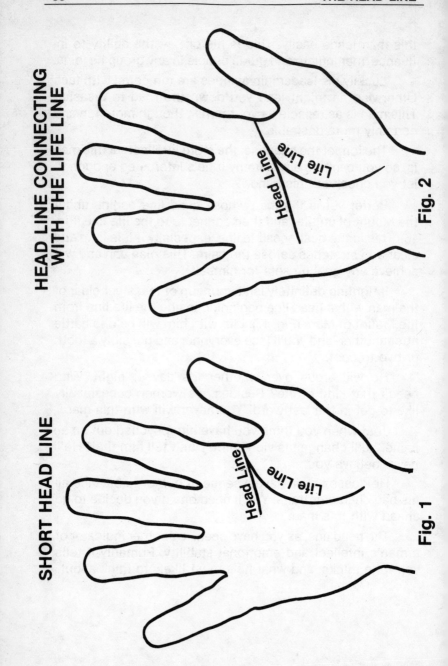

SHORT HEAD LINE

Head Line

Life Line

Fig. 1

HEAD LINE CONNECTING
WITH THE LIFE LINE

Head Line

Life Line

Fig. 2

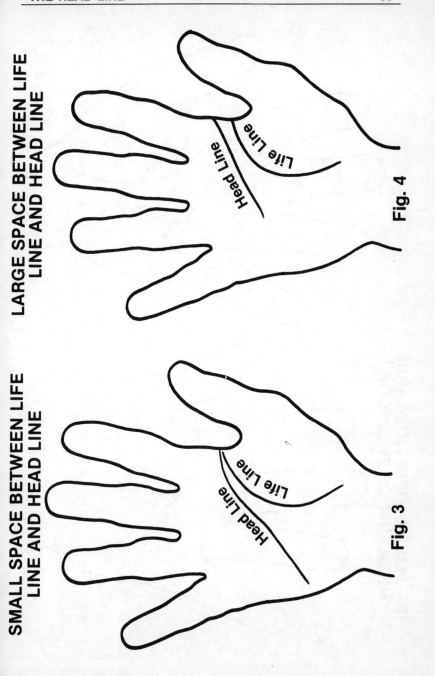

SMALL SPACE BETWEEN LIFE
LINE AND HEAD LINE

Head Line

Life Line

Fig. 3

LARGE SPACE BETWEEN LIFE
LINE AND HEAD LINE

Head Line

Life Line

Fig. 4

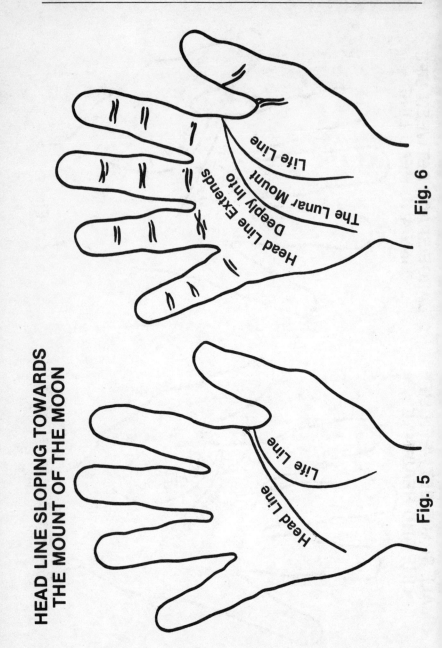

**HEAD LINE SLOPING TOWARDS THE MOUNT OF THE MOON**

Head Line Extends Deeply Into The Lunar Mount

Life Line

Fig. 6

Head Line

Life Line

Fig. 5

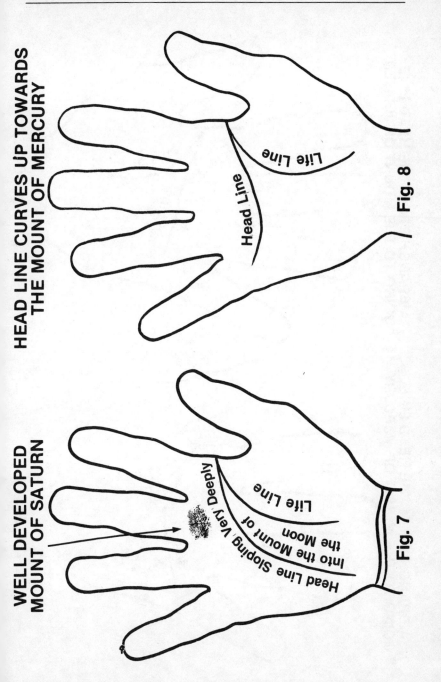

HEAD LINE CURVES UP TOWARDS
THE MOUNT OF MERCURY

Life Line

Head Line

Fig. 8

WELL DEVELOPED
MOUNT OF SATURN

Head Line Sloping Very Deeply
Into the Mount of
the Moon

Life Line

Fig. 7

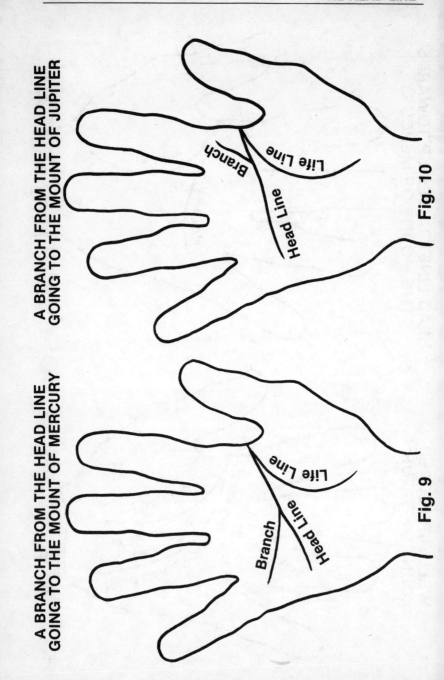

A BRANCH FROM THE HEAD LINE
GOING TO THE MOUNT OF JUPITER

Head Line

Branch

Life Line

Fig. 10

A BRANCH FROM THE HEAD LINE
GOING TO THE MOUNT OF MERCURY

Life Line

Branch

Head Line

Fig. 9

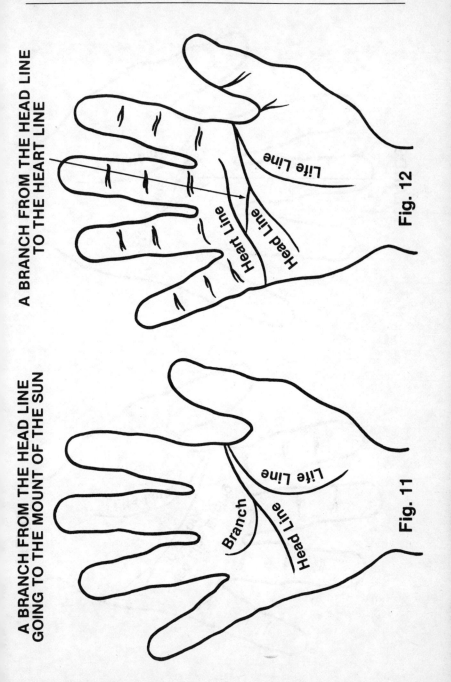

A BRANCH FROM THE HEAD LINE
TO THE HEART LINE

Heart Line

Head Line

Life Line

Fig. 12

A BRANCH FROM THE HEAD LINE
GOING TO THE MOUNT OF THE SUN

Branch

Head Line

Life Line

Fig. 11

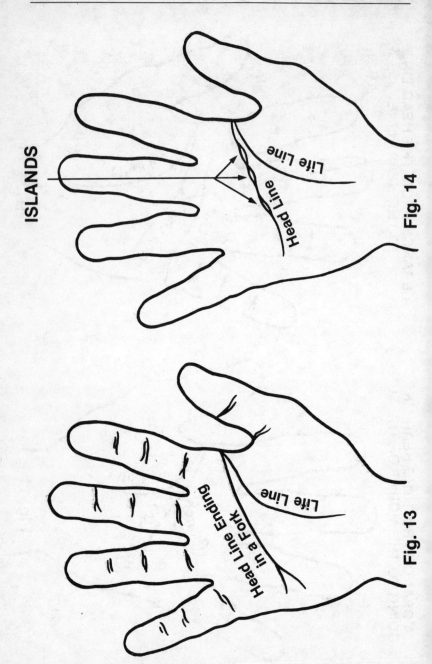

**ISLANDS**

Life Line

Head Line

Fig. 14

Head Line Ending
in a Fork

Life Line

Fig. 13

HEAD LINE STARTING FROM
THE MOUNT OF JUPITER

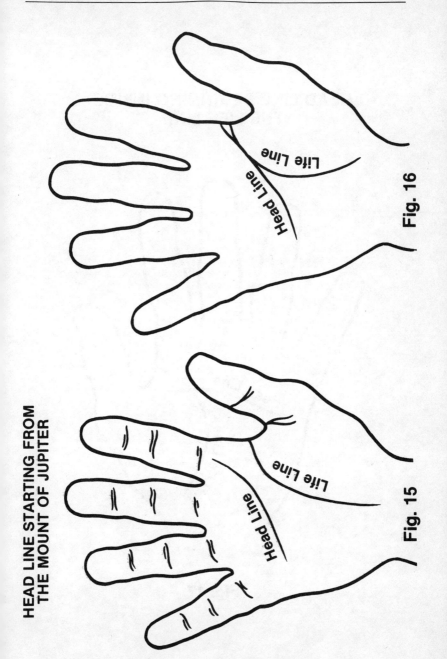

Fig. 15

Fig. 16

## HEAD LINE BEGINNING INSIDE
## THE LIFE LINE

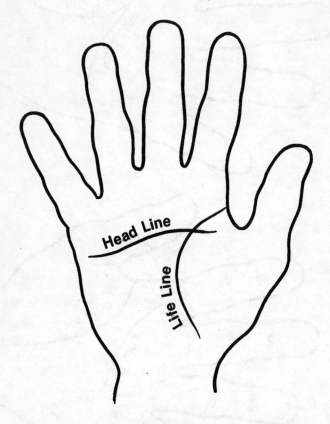

Fig. 17

# VIII.   THE HEART LINE

Each line in the hand is important, but the one of paramount importance to a woman is the heart line. This is the line that tells you a man's capacity for love.

There are obviously those who can and do love too freely. He has his opposite — the man who cannot love at all. This information is all tucked gently in his palm. Untuck it!

First, where is the heart line? You certainly can't uncover any secrets without knowing where to look. Female intuition can only take you so far...

The heart line is located at the base of the mounts, curving horizontally across the palm. It can begin and end anywhere, and these beginnings and endings are very important to you.

Where the heart line rises, under which mount, can explain many tendencies you have already observed in the men who surround you. Look carefully at the line. Does it have its beginnings under Jupiter, Saturn, The Mount of the Sun, or Mercury? Does he even have a heartline? Some men don't, you know.

You're a lucky lady if his heart line rises from the

finger of Jupiter (Fig. 1), and he whispers he's yours. This man will idolize you, or whomever wins his heart.

Lucky you, if indeed you are the one he's chosen, because he won't be able to see your faults — not one! An affectionate idealist, he's bound and determined to see his love through rose colored glasses.

If you're as smart as I think you are, you'll help maintain the rose stained illusion by becoming the woman he thinks you are. You may only be able to come close to his image, because no one is as perfect as he thinks you are.

His sole aim, once you have him in tow, is to please you. Don't do anything silly to ruin a relationship that most women would give their eye teeth to have. Remember that as long as you play the game, his every action and every thought will be geared towards your happiness. Learn to resist temptation. Otherwise one of those huntresses carefully eyeing your man will rip him off while you aren't looking. What fun is a broken heart and a cold bed?

Is passion your bag? You'll certainly find plenty of it in the man whose heart line rises below the Mount of Saturn (Fig. 2).

It is passion untempered by love. This man thinks only of his own needs, never of your fulfillment. He is always on the lookout for someone who might be able to offer him more than you offer.

If you haven't already guessed, women are his biggest weakness. He has a need to conquer as many of you as possible, but why play into his hands?

Often you can spot this type long before you become too involved. He's the fellow who takes you out to dinner then eyes every woman who enters the restaurant, mentally undressing them.

He flirts openly even though you are close to him. Marriage won't change this man. The flirtations will develop into affairs soon after the newness of marriage has worn off.

He'll use you in the bedroom to satisfy his needs when there isn't anyone else to satiate his strong physical desires. Remember, there's always a new affair right around the corner.

He can't help himself, so don't expect miracles from this man. Unhappy himself, he brings nothing but unhappiness to those who align themselves with him.

If your relationship winds up at the alter or has already, expect to hear self-recriminations when an affair is ended or he gets caught. He'll promise to change, but don't believe him. He can't. He wants to keep you around as an anchor to support him when new alliances end. Why let his self-hatred make you miserable, when all you have to do is look for a man who is compatible to your needs? Keep looking at hands and you'll find the right man for you — one who can give as well as receive.

With all his faults this man can still be a good father and a good provider. If these two items rate higher on your hunting scale than marital fidelity, you might want to consider him after all. Who's to knock a woman who goes out looking for financial security?

If this is your top priority, put on your sexiest dress, most enticing smile and go hunting.

Does his heart line begin at one side of his palm and stretch to the other side (Fig. 3)? This is the sign of extreme jealousy.

He will jump on every innocent flirtation, accusing you of desiring other men. If won't be long before you will. After all, any woman can only stand so many accusations before she begins to make them come true.

This man will expect perfection from both you and his friends. Finally everyone will tire of his constant impossible demands and look elsewhere for a friend and lover.

Until you reach that point expect his sharp temper to come into play, when either of you fail to live up to his expectations. He may regret the sharp things he has allowed his tongue to say, but the damage will already have been done.

His liking for details makes him ever more picky. It will make him a great accountant, but a lousy husband unless you are detail oriented, too.

This man will expect too much everywhere — in the office, the kitchen and the bedroom. The end results are that he makes a rotten boss, husband or lover.

The perfect heart line begins at the exact center of the Mount of Jupiter (Fig. 4). Grab, when you come across one of these.

A man whose heart line begins here, offers a love that is strong and firm. It won't waver easily when assaulted by pretty young things who know a good man when they see one. Remember, you're not the only one checking palms to find Mr. Right.

A sensitive man, he will be responsive to your needs. Warmly affectionate, his sensitivity to your desires carries over into the bedroom, where he is as desirous of your fulfillment as he is of his own.

Since you obviously won't be the only "kitty" stalking this paragon, here are a few "dos and don'ts" to follow.

Sexy clothes are out. Save them for the boudoir — after the wedding! He may want a tiger in his bedroom, but it's ladies for public display.

He needs to feel proud of the woman he chooses. Don't be afraid to show that you have a brain when you are with this man and his friends.

Now that you've been introduced to this paragon, let's shift gears and look at a very undesirable character. This is the man who has a wide, shallow, short heart line.

He lacks the human qualities of love, sympathy and understanding that every woman needs. This deficiency of feeling is accentuated if he also has a short thumb and a large Mount of Venus.

This coarse line points to a man who is more animal than human. The large Mount of Venus points to passion, but it is an animalistic passion bordering on instinctive primeval drives.

The passion is evident in the temper, too. The man, if we can call him that, who possesses a short, thick, heavy heart line is likely to fly into uncontrollable rages.

There are also men who have no heart line (Fig. 5). When a man has only one major line going from side to side, assume that the heart line is missing. The one line that is present is the head line.

This man can accomplish any goal he sets, because he isn't afraid to step on anyone, including you to get where he's going.

His shallow emotions offer you very little, though financially he may offer you tremendous gains. He will bargain for every favor he receives, so keep the stakes high to make the deal worthwhile.

He calculates every move he makes. Your dinner guests will always be someone who can benefit him, usually one step above you on the social scale.

He likes to conform to the expected norms, so don't expect to find acceptance if you march in peace rallies, demonstrate against the President, or participate in love-ins. Unless, of course, it's become the fashionable thing to do.

While this man will care little for your feelings, he cares a great deal about his. They are easily hurt, and he remembers a slight (real or imagined) for a very long time.

On the whole his relentless emotional control can goad you to do and say things you never imagined yourself doing. You'll do anything to get him to direct some emotion

— even hate — towards you. Sometimes that's all you have to prove that he is human.

Never consider finding the absence of a heart line a lucky sign, unless you, too, are a cold, calculating climber. Some of us are, you know.

One man who really enjoys being married is the man whose heart line begins on the Mount of Jupiter and is forked at its origin (Fig. 6).

Keep his home surroundings placid, because as much as he'll love you, he hates turmoil of any kind. He'll be as easy to live with as you, so set a good steady pace and the relationship has every chance of enduring permanently.

In addition to being pleasant companions and lovers, they have the added attribute of believing that no one is perfect — not even themselves.

When you find a man who has his heart line rising between the fingers of Jupiter and Saturn (Fig. 7), you have a man who is very sensible. The woman he chooses will be chosen for practical reasons. While sexual desires may, on occasion, raise their ugly head, he will never choose a wife on the basis of desire.

Mr. Common Sense and Practicality could never be accused of being a romantic. Oddly enough, his ego drives him to bed down as many women as possible.

A short heart line reveals a cool nature. Simply because this man is undemonstative in public, doesn't mean he is without feeling towards you.

He prefers to conduct his business affairs on an unemotional basis. He will not give in to your emotional appeals.

Fickle is the only word to describe the man with the chained heart line. He will flirt with any and everyone at the drop of a smile, so watch your best friend as well as him.

You will never be able to watch this fellow closely enough. Besides, guarding the home front gets to be a bore after a while.

About the only thing you can do with a fellow who likes to play guessing games is to start your own team or show him the door.

Did you like what you found in his heart line or did it depress you? This line more than any other tells you how he can relate to you and others emotionally. But again, at the risk of being boring, look at his line as only one part of his hand. The entire picture can be quite different than what one part, taken alone, implies.

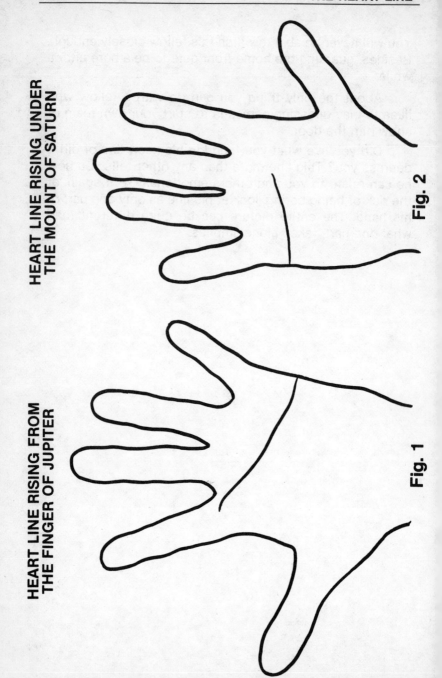

HEART LINE RISING FROM
THE FINGER OF JUPITER

Fig. 1

HEART LINE RISING UNDER
THE MOUNT OF SATURN

Fig. 2

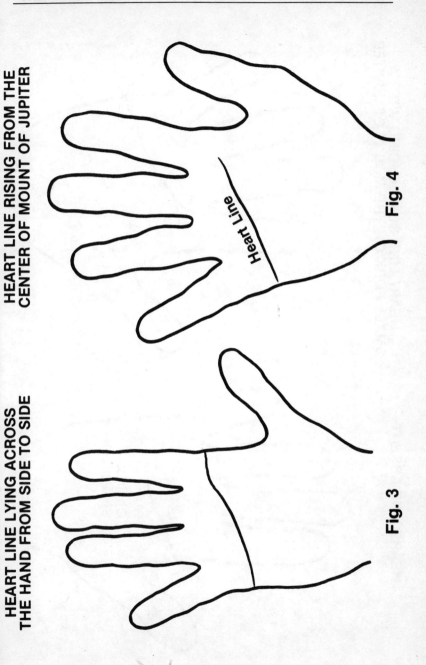

HEART LINE LYING ACROSS
THE HAND FROM SIDE TO SIDE

Fig. 3

HEART LINE RISING FROM THE
CENTER OF MOUNT OF JUPITER

Heart Line

Fig. 4

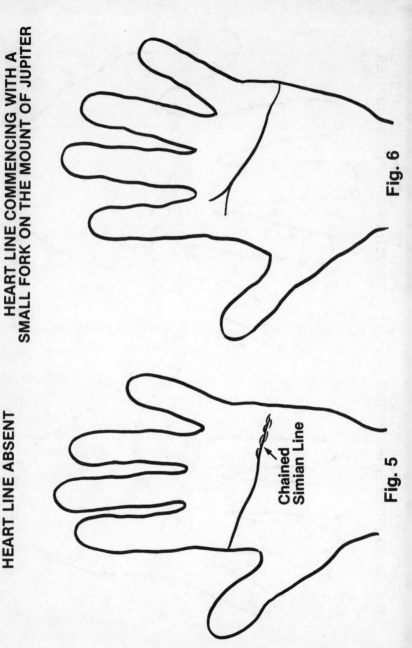

HEART LINE COMMENCING WITH A
SMALL FORK ON THE MOUNT OF JUPITER

Fig. 6

HEART LINE ABSENT

Chained
Simian Line

Fig. 5

## LINE OF HEART RISING BETWEEN THE FINGERS OF JUPITER AND SATURN

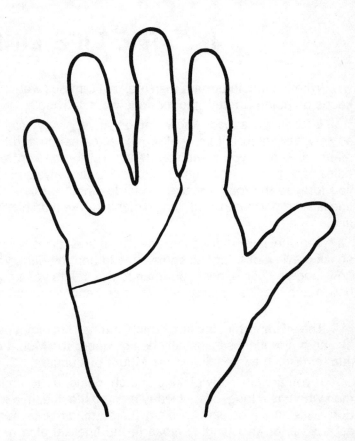

**Fig. 7**

# IX. THE LIFE LINE

What's more important than life, that tenuous web that keeps us going through the motions we call living?

Life, as you already know, can be so very, very easy or so very, very hard. If you believe in reincarnation and the reality of karma, you can understand the triumphs or tragedies each person is destined to face. Hand analysis helps you foresee the road a man's life is destined to take. No line is as important in predicting a man's future than his life line.

The life line, more than any other line, gives you a sneak preview of things to come. In addition to telling you how long you can expect your man to live, it lets you know how much medical insurance you'll need and when to buy it.

The all important life line, which outlines life expectancy and major illnesses, usually begins under the Mount of Jupiter (Fig. 1) and encircles the Mount of Venus.

If you are currently picking and choosing, try to find a man who has a long, deep, clearly marked life line. In addition make sure it doesn't have any threatening marks, such as a cross or an island. Breaks in the line are also handicaps you can do without.

Do you enjoy living dangerously? Shooting rapids on

the Colorado River...climbing El Capitan...swimming in shark infested waters...then look around until you find a man whose life, head and heart lines merge into a single line. Danger is this man's middle name. You can safely bet that a life or half a life with him will never be a bore — if you live to tell about it (Fig. 2).

Luckily for most of us a merging of the major lines is the exception rather than the rule. Generally the life line moves in one of two directions. It either sweeps gracefully around the Mount of Venus making a full arc, or it moves straight across the palm terminating on the Lunar Mount.

Health-wise the sweeping line is the more desirable of the two types (Fig. 3). In addition to getting a healthy man, you get virility thrown into the bargain.

The Mount of Venus, the hand's sexual thermometer, acts as a reservoir for the sweeping life line. The more pronounced the mount, the more it charges the current of the life line.

The straighter line tends to move through the mount rather than embracing it (Fig. 1). Unfortunately, the dissecting of the mount cuts through the man's emotional resources, crippling him.

Consequently, the man with a straight life line lacks emotional depth. The line slashes through the mount and drains off the natural warmth that normally flows from the sensual Mount of Venus. The end result will of course show up in his sexual performance, which will be cold and perfunctory. That works out perfectly providing you feel the sole purpose of sexual relations is procreation — not recreation.

You can't always judge a life line by its length. A long life line indicates longevity, but a short line doesn't guarantee a brief life span. Will power and a strong life line are a winning combination that can add an extra ten years to your man's life. Too, his life line can continue to grow and deepen.

Major events are shown chronologically and you can see them all without his even knowing what you're up to.

The more sweeping and unbroken a life line is, the more healthy the man is. Breaks are a sign of illness (Fig. 5). The chart's chronological progression will tell you if an illness has already struck home or is just waiting to happen. The secret is the "time" location of the break. If the line is full of breaks and you dislike playing Florence Nightingale, look for a better hand to hold 'til death you do part.

A break may be offset by a sister line nestling alongside the life line (Fig. 6). These lines help strengthen the ruptured main line, giving needed stability to the body.

Chains on the life line (Fig. 7) are also symptomatic of health problems, as are islands (Fig. 9). There is protection available in the form of a square. A square over an island (Fig. 8) will protect the man from a fatal illness or accident, though it won't necessarily prevent either from striking the subject.

There are other things to search for in his life line. One is a fork at the end of this vital line. (Fig. 10) The fork is a sign of power in every line but the life line. It is enough to say that is a dangerous ending to a lively line.

Tassels on the end of the life line (Fig. 9) again are a foreboding sign. The swirly tassel is a sign of weakness and destruction in any line. It is most potent in its effect on the life line.

Many lines, including the life line, send out branches. The positioning of the branches is important to their interpretation.

Branches which lift upwards from the line are a sign of strength and power. If the branch arches towards the Mount of Jupiter (Fig. 11) your man is headed on an upward course in his career at the chronological point it leaves the life line.

More good things are in store for him if a branch shoots towards the Mount of Saturn (Fig. 12), following the course of his fate line. This points to a determined man aiming at material rewards for the extra output of energy he readily gives. See, all rewards don't have to wait until you go to heaven. Besides, who says that's where you'll wind up?

When the branch ascends to the finger of Mercury (Fig. 13), your man should be a success in either science or business based on the shape of his hand.

Descending branches tell just the opposite of their upward bound sister branches. They illustrate weakness and impotency.

Another negative set of lines — there do seem to be a lot of them! — are the tiny hairlike capillary lines which run along the side of the main line. Sometimes they join the main line, while other times they fall from it, but always they drain the vital life force from the line. Like the chained formation, they denote weakness and the dissipation of the body's energy sources.

Occasionally you will find dozens of these hairlike lines twisted tightly around the life line, as they attempt to strangle the line with unknown fears. The lines are the forewarner of a nervous breakdown, so don't be surprised at the perpetual state of anxiety of this man.

Should his life line markedly divide near its termination point into two large forks (Fig. 14), his goals will also be divided.

When one fork angles towards the thumb and the other prong furrows towards the Lunar Mount, it shows that his strong desire to travel is pulling against a need to tend the home fires. He will always be pulled in both directions and occasionally will have to give in to his needs to travel. Keep a bag packed if he's your man.

Do you want a man with balance? If his head line and life line are joined at the point of origin (Fig. 3) that's a pretty strong indicator that you've found your man.

Did you think that women are the only ones who go through menopause? Think again! Men go through the same emotional and hormonal upheavals in their middle years. That time period is also marked on the life line, so expect to be as understanding of his fears of impotency as you expect him to be of your fears.

There are many myths and half truths concerning the life line...almost as many as there are about the scientific validity of hand analysis.

This chapter has dispelled some of those myths and fears, as well as increased your ability to interpret the hidden personality of the men in your life.

LIFE, HEAD AND HEART LINES
ALL JOINED TOGETHER

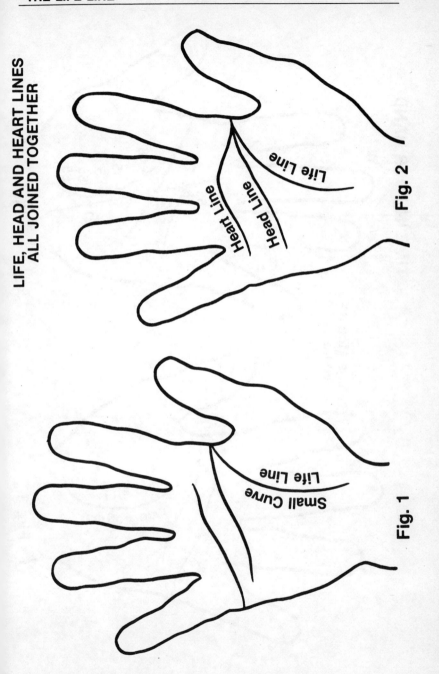

Heart Line

Head Line

Life Line

Fig. 2

Small Curve

Life Line

Fig. 1

# TIME IN YOUR HAND

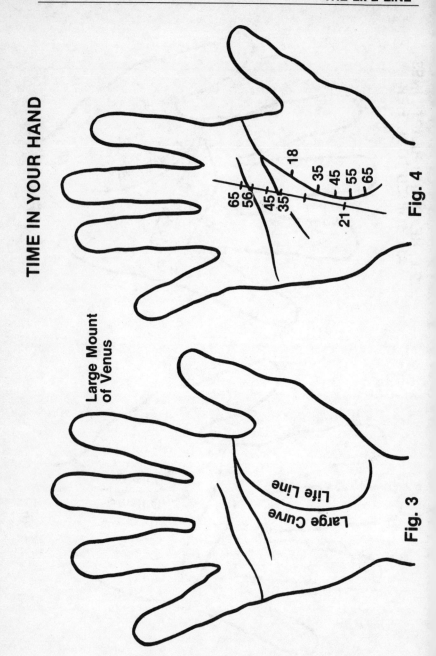

Large Mount
of Venus

Large Curve
Life Line

Fig. 3

Fig. 4

A BREAK ON THE LIFE LINE

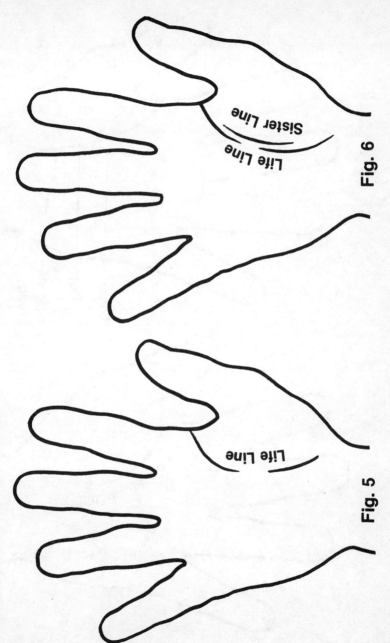

Fig. 6

Life Line

Sister Line

Fig. 5

Life Line

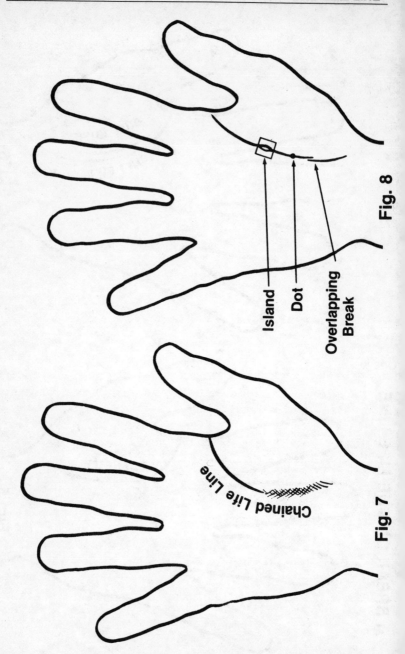

Island

Dot

Overlapping
Break

Fig. 8

Chained Life Line

Fig. 7

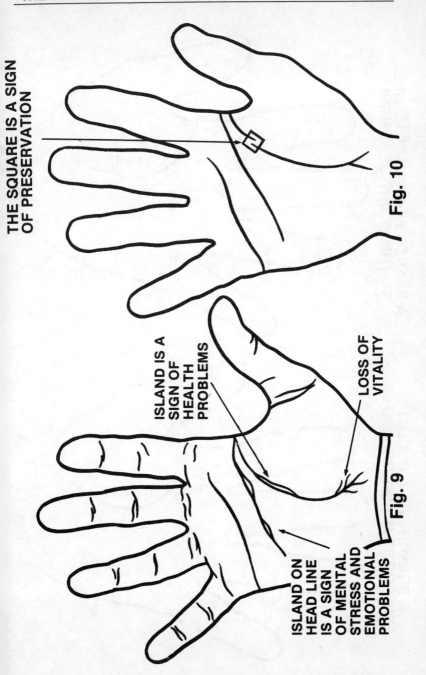

THE SQUARE IS A SIGN OF PRESERVATION

Fig. 10

ISLAND IS A SIGN OF HEALTH PROBLEMS

LOSS OF VITALITY

ISLAND ON HEAD LINE IS A SIGN OF MENTAL STRESS AND EMOTIONAL PROBLEMS

Fig. 9

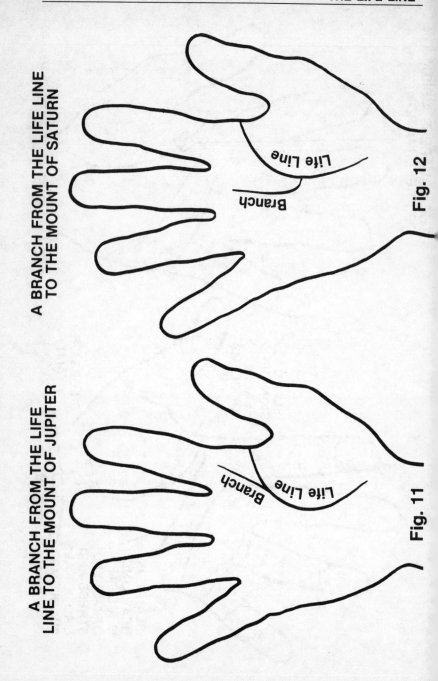

A BRANCH FROM THE LIFE LINE TO THE MOUNT OF JUPITER

Fig. 11

A BRANCH FROM THE LIFE LINE TO THE MOUNT OF SATURN

Fig. 12

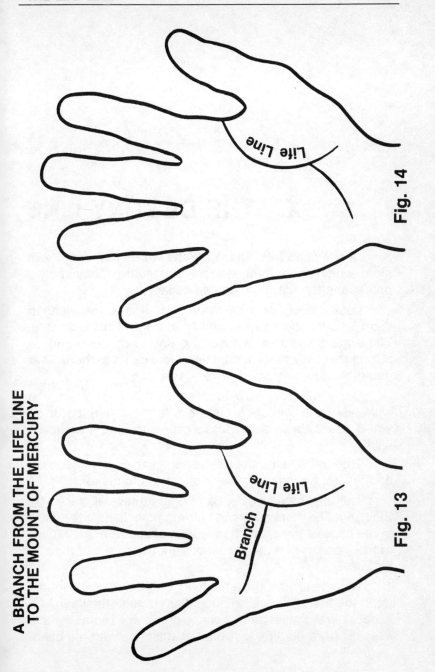

A BRANCH FROM THE LIFE LINE
TO THE MOUNT OF MERCURY

Branch

Life Line

Fig. 13

Life Line

Fig. 14

# X. THE DESTINY LINE

Destiny and fate...these are the words that conjure visions which are both mysterious and illusive. They imply a predestination that no man can escape.

Look closely at a man's destiny line if you want to learn whether he has the ability to control his own fate. There are some men whose fate line is so deep and so strong that they must accept what fate deals to them. That could be very, very good or very, very bad.

Once you learn how to interpret the destiny line you will know what direction his life will take. Then it's up to you if you want to share fate's ride with him. It could be wild!

True to its name the destiny line shows both success and failure, tragedy and major shifts in life style.

The line, being fickle, can begin at several places on the hand. The most common starting point is near the wrist at the base of the palm. It may also begin from the Mount of the Moon, inside the Mount of Venus or at any of the major lines.

There is always the possibility that the line will not exist in the hand you are holding. Even though this man is a success in the most narrow sense of the word something is missing from his life, just as it is missing from his hand.

Maybe he subconsciously sought you out because you have a strong destiny line — that's what usually happens with men who have no destiny line of their own.

Let's assume he does have a destiny line. Check out its possibilities.  First, where does it start?

If the fate line begins at the Mount of the Moon (Fig. 1), look out. This is a very sound indication that he is both a leaner and a taker.

A man whose destiny line begins at the Mount of the Moon usually can't make it on his own. He needs other people to push him into whatever success he will achieve. He knows all of the angles to getting pushed onwards and upwards.

You may happen to like to be the main thrust behind your man. If that's the case and you have what appear to you to be excellent ideas for getting him to the top, more power to you.

This man isn't all bad.  Not only does he like women, he likes to be influenced by them. In more ways than one...if you like to be in the driver's seat, drive on!

When you choose to spend more time with this man, expect to spend it in the glare of the spotlight. If you haven't noticed, he needs the warmth of the public — any public — to feel secure.

When the crowds have all gone home, you will have to provide the extra warmth he usually gets from them.  While you cuddle and cuddle him, continue to influence him in the direction you want him to go.

Expect to play many roles. This man is an actor on and off the stage, so you'll have to know his moods and play them to your advantage.

One minute you will be expected to be a brave, long-suffering Desdemona, while your Othello struts and sputters across the stage making vile accusations. The next you must be Juliet, succumbing to the suddenly innocent love-making of a man who will always be part child. All because his destiny line begins at the Mount of the Moon...

If you desire stability in both your life and your man, find one whose destiny line begins at the wrist (Fig. 2) and has no bad marks importuning the line. It should run straight from the wrist to the Mount of Saturn.

His only problem may be that he is an independent cuss and has been for a long time. This only adds to his stability and determination to achieve his goals — you make it a problem if you can't accept it. He, unlike many men, is master of his own destiny and he knows it.

In addition to being goal-oriented he likes people, including you. If you're one of his goals, look out — remember he's the master of his own destiny. If you like, let his destiny win and blame fate.

He adapts easily to changes, such as from bachelorhood to marriage. There's only one catch to this paragon — there are all too few of them. Remember, you're not the only woman on his trail.

Does your man's fate line begin at the life line (Fig. 3) and run to the Mount of Saturn? It's very likely that this man lacked a showcase for his various talents when he was younger. The more mature he becomes, the more likely these buried talents will emerge from their hiding place.

This is also a man who will be close to his family, and that could mean you. He will be less likely to stray, than say, the man whose fate line begins at the Lunar Mount. He doesn't need hundreds of admirerers to tell him how wonderful he is through their applause and their bodies. One good woman suffices for this man; or occasionally one bad woman, if she hides it well enough.

Does the man you're most interested in, get everything he has by struggling and fighting? More than likely his destiny line rises from the head line (Fig. 4). The deeper the line, the more prone he will be to achieve some degree of success later in life. Do you want to wait until you may be too old to enjoy the benefits of the success? That's the question.

Is having a man around to take care of you in your old age of prime importance to you? The man whose fate line begins at the heart line (Fig. 5) will be able to do this. He should achieve success just in time — old age.

There are things to offset the potency of the line's birthplace. First, to be a true indicator the line must be deep, long and strong. Many lines begin strongly, but like some sexual partners, don't produce in the long run.

A man who has a strong overall hand with a dominant, deep destiny line has that something extra that guarantees he'll be a winner. Your best bet, if you come across a man with a destiny line like this, is to grab him while he's young. His shelf life is very short.

Are you more masochistic by nature? Do you both need and desire a dominant man? Then, a man with a strong destiny line and a larger than average thumb is just what the psychiatrist would order.

These men love to dominate. The people they love to dominate most are women. If you really dislike domineering men, then that's another battle, you may find yourself missing a few teeth if you marry one. Despite all the feminist rhetoric, almost any male, on occasion, will deck almost any woman. A few Amazons can hold their own.

Many a man may be successful in the accepted sense and seemingly strong, but something will definitely be missing if he has a weak destiny line. Financial successes like this usually manage to find themselves a woman with a strong fate line. This woman may be a wife, a mistress or even his mother.

Do you want your man to be healthy, wealthy and wise? And why not? Then search out the fellow who has both a strong fate line and a strong sun line (Fig. 6).

Marry a man with these two powerful lines and you'll never wind up as a permanent nursemaid in your sunset years.

Regardless of what many books on palmistry and hand analysis say, a strong deep destiny line is not a passport to a successful career — but it sure helps a lot. Part of the reason is that these men have the ability to adjust to changing circumstances and environs more quickly than others. They take advantage of this ability.

This man is determined to make the best of everything. You know the kind of guy...he's the one who gets a lemon and winds up making darn good lemonade. The kind of man women love and men envy...

If this is your man, he definitely has his head on straight and knows right where he's going. Again, if he doesn't quite reach his goal he can accept the fact that maybe he aimed too high. He won't complain about life dealing him a poor hand, because he knows and accepts himself for what he is — a man.

Again, a destiny line alone doesn't insure instant success for a man. It does tell me and will tell you other things that are important to you about your man.

This tell-tale line marks such as childhood traumas, major love affairs, financial status, divorces, accidents — everything except how many drinks he had with the boys last night. The events are marked chronologically (Fig. 7) as they happened or will happen.

Something that gives added zest to any man's hand is the convergence of the four major lines into a capital "M" (Fig. 8). This is a sure sign that fate shines on this man. If he is fortunate enough to have this sign in both hands he gets a double dose of Lady Luck.

Among other things the "M" signals emotional maturity. It shows a man who can make his own decisions without your help, but at least he'll have the good sense to pretend to listen.

This man knows what he wants for himself, even better than you do. He proves it by often succeeding at getting what he wants, doesn't he? He isn't about to have anyone else run his life — a mother figure is not what he wants.

A cross (Fig. 9-A) on the line can spell trouble for your man, which in turn might spell trouble for you. The trouble might already have hit. In that case you have nothing to worry about. Check the line against the life line to determine if you have anything to worry about.

If the trouble still looms in the future you're at least aware that it will strike, and when it will hit. This makes it easier for you to prepare and be ready with a helping hand and maybe more.

Besides that same cross or any other negative sign can be offset by a square (Fig. 9-B) on the same line. Squares are the insurance policies of hand analysis, offering sure fire protection at no extra cost to the policy holder.

Like the old river captains you have to watch out for islands (Fig. 9-C). They can be very dangerous to your health, but again a magic square in the right spot can protect you. To know when a health problem will arise, check the age at which the island appears, using the previous chart.

Crossbars on the lines foretell obstacles. Close observation of the mounts and major lines should tell you what types of obstacles to expect.

There is nothing bright in the star you might find on his destiny line (Fig. 9-D). It shows a traumatic experience either in his past or his future, and if the star is on the Mount of Saturn the experience will be even more traumatic.

Don't panic if you find a star dissecting the fate line, especially if the line continues past the star. This is a sign that he will weather the storm. Time is the primary factor.

The deeper and stronger the line is as it moves out from the star, the more quickly your man will recover his losses.

What about the line itself? What does it look like? Is it long and deep as a good destiny line should be, or is it weak and shallow? Is it one straight line or is it broken? What about branches? Which way do they go? These, too, affect you man's destiny.

A thin irregular destiny line is like an irregular heart beat, and should be watched just as closely. These breaks signal change. Some of the changes are planned and generally work out well. It's the dramatic unexpected changes (unexpected unless you see them with the palmist's trained eyes) to look out for.

A clear break in his hand is a sound predictor of a storm, which you may or may not want to weather with him. If you think he's worth the trouble, even though there are numerous breaks in the destiny line, be prepared for stormy weather

Your one savior is a square over the broken area to protect him. It will be especially helpful in easing the strain of a career upset and/or marital problems.

During the period affected by the break, don't expect too many smiles. He will exist going through the routine of living until the break heals and fate shines again.

Are the breaks softened by overlapping lines? The overlapping lines still mean change, but the changes will be planned in advance. You and he will plan these changes together, so they will not have the same cutting effect on your lives as a clean break would bave.

Still there is the element of chance, but then isn't that what life is all about? The wider the overlap, the more difficult a time the man will have adjusting to the change.

Some people also have a double fate line. Lucky him, instead of one career he'll have two distinct careers! He certainly will never be bored, but you might go berserk trying to keep up with this two-time winner. His hand will be even more impressive if the fate lines go to two different mounts.

Often the way a destiny line terminates is just as important as its beginnings and meanderings on the palm. Determine where his destiny line ends, then continue reading.

If it terminates at the Mount of the Sun, this man is likely to do anything, including criminal activities, to bask in the public spotlight. He needs to feed on the adulation of others. His talents usually provide him the adulation he thrives on.

You will have to help him make tough decisions, because he will be beset with inner conflicts over the material versus artistic aspects of his life. If you work the game right, he can often have both.

What can you expect if your man's destiny line sweeps to a generous curve ending at the forefinger? Politics here you come, because this is the name of the game for this fellow.

He will almost definitely be drawn into either legislative, public, administrative or corporate politics. He loves the pressured wheeling and dealing that make the political game so exciting.

He can be a tough taskmaster at home and at work, but the excitement of being part of his inner circle makes the pressure worthwhile. If it doesn't, you'd better take your knitting and look for a more complacent, dull fellow.

Excitement can get some men into trouble, especially when the excitement comes from an overactive libido and an underactive brain. The man who doesn't plan his affairs carefully can wind up in lots of hot water — many a politician has learned that to his detriment! His tendencies toward wine and women will be well known to you if you look at his hand carefully.

The man whose destiny line stops abruptly at the heart line will probably mess up his career through tantalizing but stupid affairs. Women, especially beautiful women, are too important and influential for his own good.

If his destiny line terminates at the head line, fate has something else unpleasant in store for him. He is the man whom success always eludes, because his calculations are always just a hair off.

The destiny line will often have branches shooting off to the various mounts. Each branch is important, taking on the characteristics of the mount it touches.

What destiny is there for the unfortunate man who has no destiny line? He can succeed. Usually his personal life always seems to have something missing. He is not a happy man, since others recognize his emptiness. He cannot relate well. He can be helped by a woman who possesses a strong destiny line and decides to share her fate with him.

Fate...Destiny...They're not quite so mysterious now that you know how to read them in the palms of the men who are important to you. Your knowledge can help change their destiny and yours.

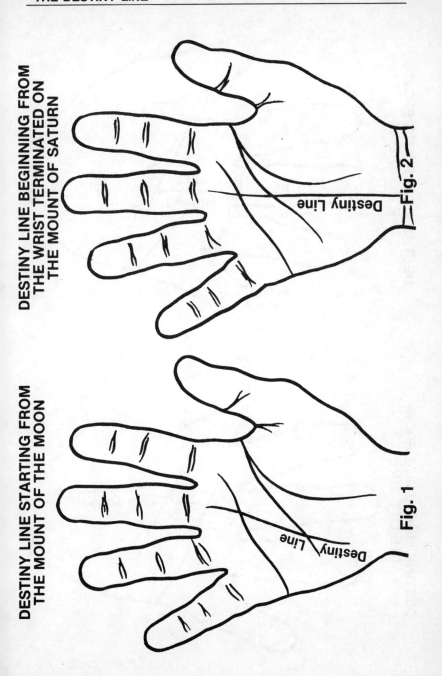

DESTINY LINE STARTING FROM THE MOUNT OF THE MOON

Destiny Line

Fig. 1

DESTINY LINE BEGINNING FROM THE WRIST TERMINATED ON THE MOUNT OF SATURN

Destiny Line

Fig. 2

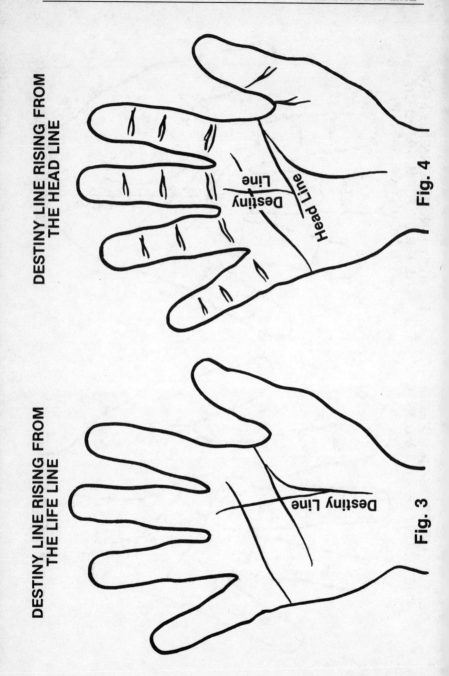

DESTINY LINE RISING FROM
THE LIFE LINE

Destiny Line

Fig. 3

DESTINY LINE RISING FROM
THE HEAD LINE

Destiny
Line

Head Line

Fig. 4

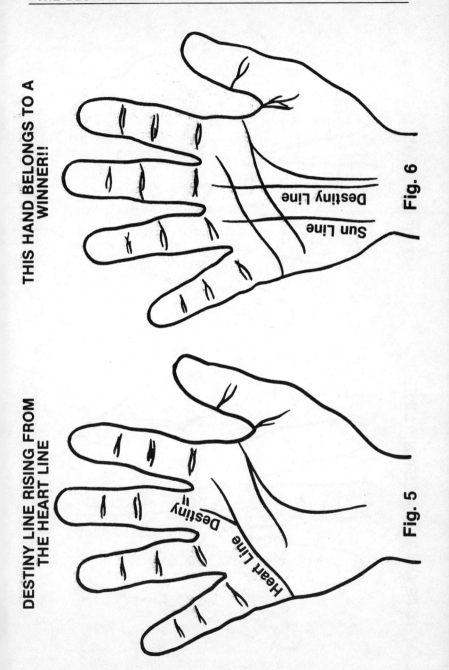

DESTINY LINE RISING FROM
THE HEART LINE

Heart Line

Destiny

Fig. 5

THIS HAND BELONGS TO A
WINNER!!

Destiny Line

Sun Line

Fig. 6

# TIME ON THE DESTINY LINE

# THE BIG "M"

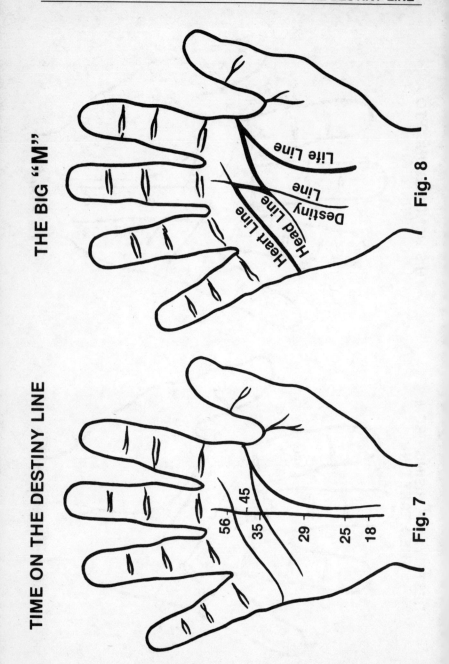

Fig. 7

Fig. 8

56
45
35
29
25
18

Heart Line

Head Line

Destiny Line

Life Line

# MARKS ON THE DESTINY LINE

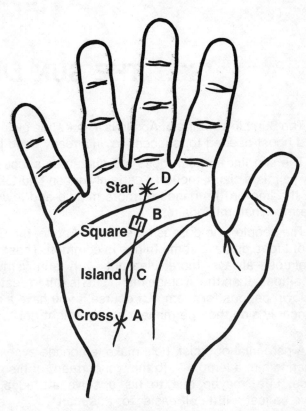

**Fig. 9**

# XI.   THE SUN LINE

The Sun Line or Line of Apollo is a lucky line giving the added boost needed for success to an already good hand.

The sun line in itself does not guarantee success as many palmists claim, though it certainly doesn't hurt. I have seen the line on the hands of more middle and lower income men than millionaires.

The people who possess the line of Apollo, the Greek God of Light, do have some things in common. These men are almost always more pleasant with sunnyside up dispositions, than the average man. Life is full fo zest with few down periods for them. Of course if you have a more melancholy side their permanent smiles might get to be a drag.

A perennial optimist, he'll make lemonade every time life hands him a lemon — to the wonderment of his many friends. Life, maybe due to his positive attitudes, will always be just a little bit easier for this man.

Good sun lines come in pairs — one to a hand. He can have as many as three sun lines indicative of potential success in several fields.

If he is limited to one sun line (Fig. 1), which is still better than no sun line, note which hand has the line. A line on the left hand holds the promise but not the guarantee of success.

If he only has a sun line on his right hand and is right-handed, the outlook for success in whatever field he chooses is more positive.

The man without a sun line is to be pitied. No matter how talented these men are they rarely fulfill the potential of their talents — at least not during their lifetime. Often their genius is recognized after their death.

A surefire winner is one who has a long deep sun line in each hand, a long destiny line (Fig. 2), long head line and a large strong thumb. Again, these fellows are few and far between, but that shouldn't stop you from looking.

Where the line has its origin is also very important. A line starting from the wrist (Fig.3) and running to the Mount of the Sun is a sign of success and achievement (Fig. 1).

If it starts from the Mount of the Moon (Fig. 4) the degree of success will be on the shoulders of others, instead of the man whose hand you should be holding, if you're not. Remember practice in a lot of areas makes perfect.

Does the line begin from the destiny line (Fig. 5)? It may be a full-fledged sun line, but then again it may only be a branch of the destiny line. Either way it adds to his potential for a successful career and happiness, so why knock it?

A sun line, which begins at the Mount of Mars (Fig. 6), is a symbol of aggressiveness, ambition and the need to succeed in public life. That's a far cry from the usual sunny projections from this line.

Sometimes the sun line has its origins in the head line (Fig. 7). This is a man who will use his brain to achieve his goals. The success is almost certain but it will take until middle age to achieve it. Better late than never — as long as you know it's there, right?

An even later achiever is the man who has a sun line which originates at the heart line (Fig. 8). Whatever success he has will not come until late in life.

Just as the starting position of the line is important, so are the various marks that can add or detract from the sign's potency.

Islands, as always, are bad news. (Fig. 9-A). On the sun line they indicate a loss of money or reputation. A juicy scandal is often indicated by an island, but like all else in life it will pass.

His reputation can also be damaged by a small cross (Fig. 9-B) on the sun line.

These two potentially damaging marks can be offset by our old standby, the square (Fig. 9-C). It will protect him from people who would destroy his reputation through jealousy.

Believe it or not the star (Fig. 9-d), a curse on other lines, is a good luck sign, when it is located on the sun line.

The sun line is not considered a major line, and its absence does not hinder a man's ambitions, especially if his goal is any sort of public position. One long line on the Major hand is good, but a pair is even better.

# THE SUN LINE

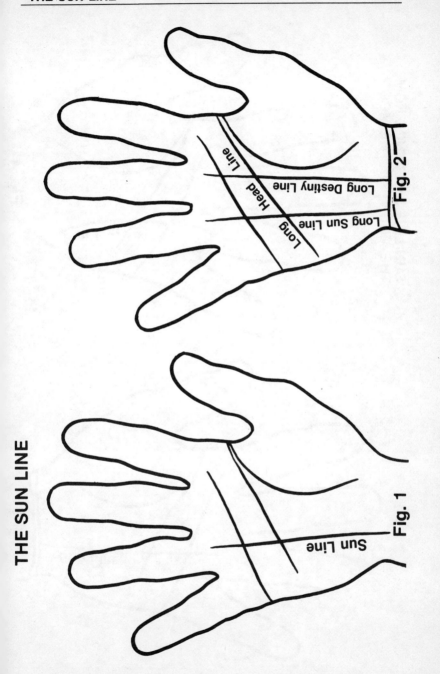

Sun Line

Fig. 1

Long Sun Line
Long Head
Line
Long Destiny Line

Fig. 2

SUN LINE STARTING FROM
THE MOUNT OF THE MOON

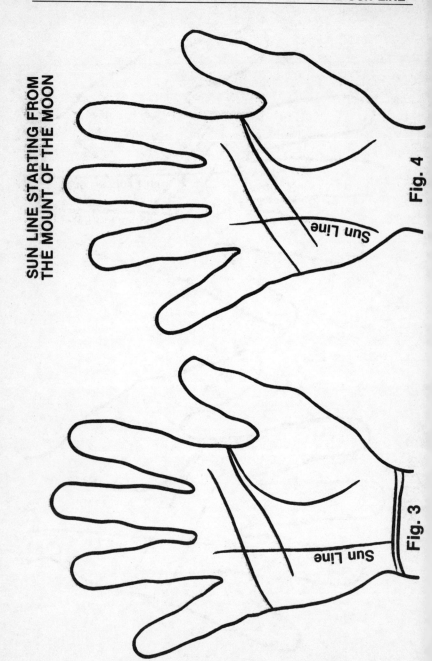

Sun Line

Fig. 4

Sun Line

Fig. 3

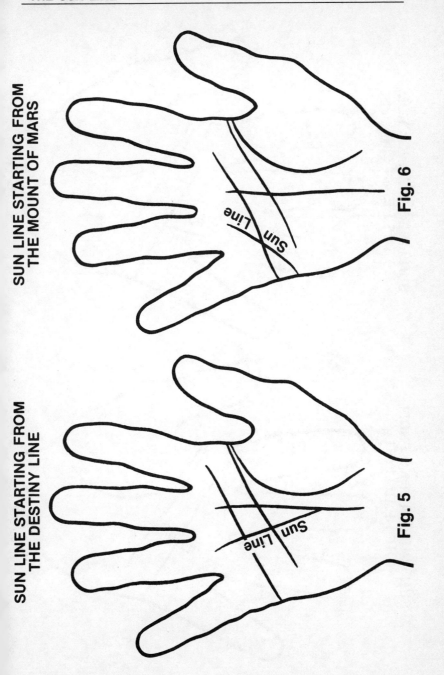

SUN LINE STARTING FROM THE DESTINY LINE

Fig. 5

SUN LINE STARTING FROM THE MOUNT OF MARS

Fig. 6

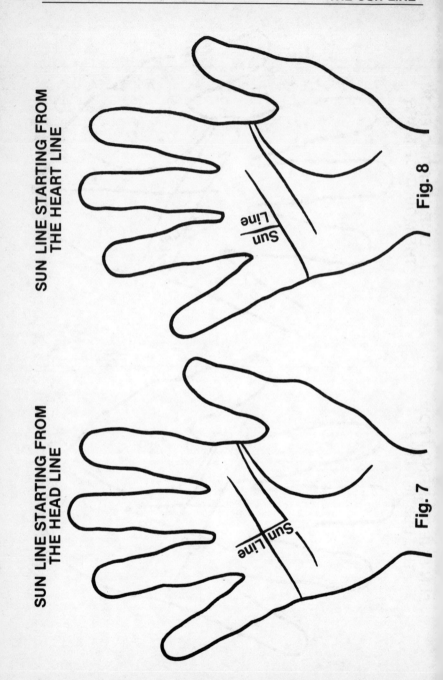

SUN LINE STARTING FROM THE HEAD LINE

Sun Line

Fig. 7

SUN LINE STARTING FROM THE HEART LINE

Sun Line

Fig. 8

# MARKS ON THE SUN LINE

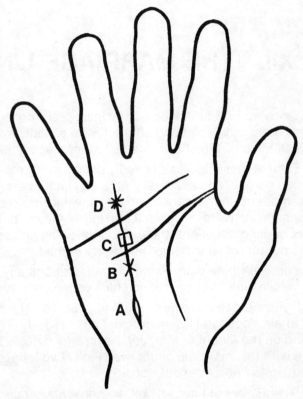

**Fig. 9**

# XII.  THE MARRIAGE LINES

Once upon a time when all women were considered pure in more than spirit and all men were gallant, what we now call lines of affection were called marriage lines.

Each of these lines supposedly designated a marriage, because no one, and especially females, had affairs. Now, we're modern and adult and accept the fact that almost everyone has an affair — even if it's only in the mind. These affairs or deep affections show up on the palm, just as marriages do, though maybe not as deeply etched.

You can't hide your own little indiscretions any more than he can, unless of course you hide your palmistry book.

If you want to discover the fate of your marriage or current affair, look at HIS marriage lines (Fig. 1). They're located on the Mount of Mercury. As an added guide to the future with this man, you might even look at your lines — it does help to know yourself, too.

The number of lines will tell you how many marriages and major affairs this man has had and will have. Talk about tell tale lines! The lines will also tell when these events did or will happen.

Does a marriage line snuggle up close to his heart

line? If it does, he got into the love and marriage game very early, somewhere between the ages of 15 and 21.

A slow starter, a second marriage or love affair is indicated when a marriage line moves toward the center of the Mount of Mercury. If the line on his hand moves in this direction, his heart and his paycheck will be captured between the ages of 21 and 28.

When the line travels three quarters of the way up the mount, it indicates a love between the ages of 28 and 35. You can plot the time table and your own campaign best by comparing the line with the chronological chart of the life line and destiny line.

The longer and deeper the lines are, the more likely they represent actual marriage complete with a signed contract — not the sex games that are so popular today.

If the timing shown on his hand isn't right for you, but you want him anyway, go ahead and play the game. Remember games are fun, but each one has a winner and more importantly a loser. When the fun and games are over, no tears, please! That's one of the cardinal rules of adult game playing.

A good marriage line should be straight without breaks, crosses, stars and other irregularities (Fig. 1-E) that upset the honeymoon fervor of married life.

Small crosses are all right for him to have on a marriage line, but they may prove fatal to the woman in his life. A small cross covering the curve of a downward line is a sure indicator of accidental or sudden death involving someone he loves — hopefully not you.

Islands on the marriage line are hazards (Fig. 2-A), just as they are on any other line. During the space of time the island rests in the middle of his marriage line, there will definitely be troubles on the matrimonial seas.

If you can hold on long enough the waves will simmer down. Maybe you don't want to wait for the high water mark to drop. Divorce does happen you know — even the best people do it! Who's to say the life of a divorcee isn't better than martyrdom with an alcoholic or a philanderer?

This is a decision you might not have to make if you look at his hand closely before you become too involved. Regardless of what you think now, all marriages aren't made in heaven — quite a few are filled with hellfire and brimstone. It's there in the palm for you to see. The final decision always rests with you.

The more islands on the lines, the more hazards you will have in establishing a fulfilling relationship. There are real problems when the islands are combined with downward sloped marriage lines. A man with this type of a marriage line is incapable of sharing happiness, so unless you like to cry a lot, look elsewhere for a man.

There will be similar difficulties in any relationship where one or more lines end in a fork (Fig. 2-B). Love at your own risk is what these lines tell you, Lady.

Breaks in the marriage line are unhealthy for love (Fig. 2-C), just as breaks in a fate line are bad for a man's career. The break points to a sudden shattering split in the relationship, which will be almost impossible to mend.

A distinct marriage line with small hairlike lines dropping from it as it moves toward the heartline points to trouble. Those are lines you could probably live without.

Should the marriage line move upwards and into the Mount of the Sun (Fig. 3-D), your fellow's in luck. It's a sure sign he will marry or at least consort with a lady of distinction. He gets other bonuses with a package like that, because the lady will be famous or wealthy or both. Is that you?

Downward lines bring negative attributes, and when a marriage line cuts down through the sun line it can bring a fellow to his knees fast (Fig. 3-E). Marriage or even an affair will cost him in both money and position, a high price to pay for a bad line.

When you spot a line growing down and out of the marriage line, flowing from the top of the mount (Fig. 3-G), be aware that there will be an organized opposition to his forming a lasting relationship. Figure out where the opposition will come from and plan your own counterattack if he's worth the effort.

Are there fine lines running parallel with and almost touching the marriage line (Fig. 3-F)? If there are, look for him to become very affectionate with someone after his marriage — it's not you. It definitely is someone else and the relationship will be very strong.

Good deep lines indicate that the man can and will give great physical satisfaction. He has to have a partner who is his sexual equal at home or elsewhere.

Branches rising from the marriage lines foretell a warm affectionate relationship that can survive the day to day friction of marriage. Just the opposite is true if the branches turn downward.

Should you find a dot on his marriage line, regard it as a blemish on the love he offers. The relationship will not last, and the exact termination will depend on how the line ends. If it terminates in a tassel, all emotional ties will be severed quickly and completely — for him at least.

Should the line begin thinning out gradually from the dot, the ties will slowly dissolve. In the long run a slow break can be more painful than a quick blow.

What if he doesn't have a marriage line? It means no woman, including you, will dent his armor. He uses women to fill his physical needs, but he has no more affection for them than for a cat or dog that might live in his house.

When there are no marriage lines and he also has a short heart line, he may marry, but only for convenience. He still likes a warm meal and clean house, and that's what a wife is for, isn't it?

A good marriage and good strong marriage line never hurt anyone. In fact, many people feel that both contribute to a person's longevity. In other words, if you want to live a long life, love a lot — but with the same person.

MARRIAGE LINES

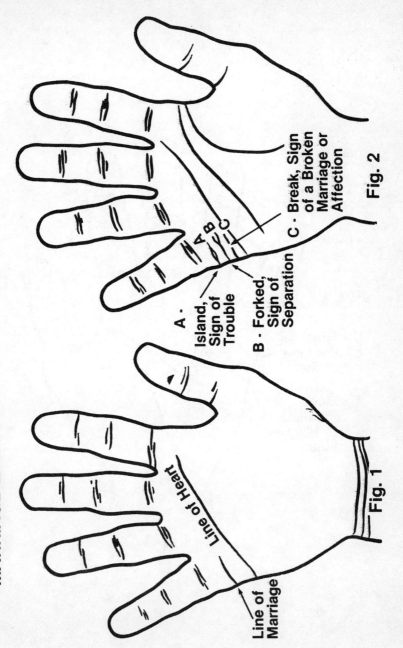

A - Island, Sign of Trouble

B - Forked, Sign of Separation

C - Break, Sign of a Broken Marriage or Affection

Line of Heart

Line of Marriage

Fig. 1

Fig. 2

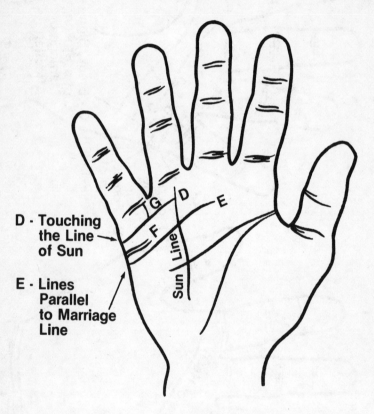

D - Touching
the Line
of Sun

E - Lines
Parallel
to Marriage
Line

**Fig. 3**

# CONCLUSION

Now that you have completed the book, let it be a new beginning. If you have read, accepted and absorbed what I've written, you'll never again look at a man's face before you look at his hand.

A face can be taught to lie, but it is impossible for the hands to be untruthful. What they have to tell you, was etched there by a force far greater than any single individual and only that force can change what it has written.

Never judge a man by a single part of his hand. Always remember that every bad sign can be mellowed by a strong point elsewhere in the hand. It is the palm in its totality, as well as the fingers, that give us the insights into a man's character we need for our own protection.

Don't expect to be an instant expert. Continue your studies knowing that the old proverb, "a little knowledge is a dangerous thing," holds true for hand analysis, too.

Don't grab any man just because he is willing. Learn to know yourself, so that you know the kind of man who best fills your needs. Then begin your search, and remember, you'll know him first by his hands.

## "Good Luck"